REENTRY & TRANSITION

PLANNING CIRCLES FOR INCARCERATED PEOPLE

Lorenn Walker & Rebecca Greening

Reentry & Transition Planning Circles for Incarcerated People

by Lorenn Walker & Rebecca Greening

First Print Edition

© Copyright 2011 - Walker & Greening

ISBN-13: 978-0615529424

Published by Hawai'i Friends of Justice & Civic Education

Hawai'i, USA

www.hawaiifriends.org

Table of Contents

All proceeds from the sale of this book will benefit the work of

Hawaiʻi Friends of Justice & Civic Education

www.hawaiifriends.org a U.S. 501(c)(3) nonprofit

Acknowledgments

We are grateful to many who have supported this work including the Hawai'i Friends of Justice & Civic Education and the Wallace Alexander Gerbode Foundation, all past and current board members who have enthusiastically helped; the late Insoo Kim Berg, co-founder of solution-focused brief therapy who assisted in designing the Circles; Australian professor, author, and peace activist John Braithwaite for suggesting transition planning as a restorative process; Shadd Maruna law professor, Queens University, Ireland for sharing his extensive criminal desistance knowledge; Kat Brady a tireless community justice advocate who saw incarcerated people could benefit from restorative reentry; Ted Sakai a former prison warden and director of the Hawai'i state prison system who understood the value of this reentry and transition planning process and assisted with piloting it at Waiawa prison in 2004; Mark Patterson warden of the Hawai'i Women's Community Correctional Center for trying to make prison a place where people heal; Phil Zimbardo, Stanford professor and trail blazer who has helped educate the world on the need for humanizing correctional programs; James Richardson professor at Shidler School of Business, University of Hawai'i, Carolyn Kampf UC Davis, and Peggy Ireland of Canada for editorial assistance; all others who provided ideas or support for this work including Gale Burford, Katherine van Wormer, Peter Dejong, Adriana Uken, Marina Cantacuzino, Marilia Duffles, Edwina Grosvenor, Linda Mills, Kay Pranis, Barbara Turdor, Sunny Schwartz, Ben Furman, Ted Wachtel, Howard Zehr, Dan Van Ness, Dorothy Roberts, Albert Bandura, Daniel Goleman, Carol Tavris, Ellen Langer, Jill Taylor, Jeremy Travis, the Offender Aid and Restoration of Arlington County, Inc., the Vera Institute for Justice; all Hawai'i state prison staff and administrators who supported or participated in the Circles, provided insight and helped arrange them; the Hawai'i Judiciary and its judges; the Hawai'i Legislature; finally, we are deeply thankful to the incarcerated individuals and their loved ones whose courage to face their pain and find solutions, continually inspire us.

Lorenn is especially grateful to Rebecca Greening, brilliant young lawyer, former New York University social work student, and tenacious Boston Latin School graduate, who saw early in her career the need for restorative justice approaches to deal with crime and social problems. Lorenn is also hugely grateful for Dawn Slaten and Diane Stowell for their help with this and other restorative justice and solution-focused programs over the years.

Foreword

Critically missing from virtually all corrections systems around our nation are programs that effectively prepare incarcerated people released from prison directly, being paroled, and those coming out of residential substance abuse programs, to reenter society and transition back as responsible citizens. That is why I am so enthusiastic about this new workbook that utilizes a dynamic strategy based on public health, social psychology, mentoring, restorative justice, solution-focused brief therapy, etc., in creating community Circles to enable such vital transitions to work for the target individuals, their social support members, as well as the prison community.

Lorenn Walker and Rebecca Greening have combined their long experience in the corrections arena with big picture wisdom and a fine-grained tactical focus in designing these "planning circles for incarcerated people." This highly readable book blends interesting case studies with detailed practical formula for how to create such Circle processes, and equally important how to assess their validity. The exorbitant monetary and psychological costs of high recidivism rates across our juvenile justice system, jails, and prisons merits a careful appraisal of this attempt to correct and reverse that recurring societal failure. I endorse the widest possible utilization of this program, and the application of these wise principles to empower formerly imprisoned people to take charge of their lives with the help of family, friends, and prison staff.

Phil Zimbardo
San Francisco, California
April 2011

For every prisoner returning home, we should ask this question, "What will it take to keep this prisoner from committing another crime or being the victim of a crime? In essence, we should create a safety plan for each prisoner to provide a safe transition over the first few months following release."

- Jeremy Travis[1]

Preface

This book describes a reentry and transition group planning process for incarcerated people to guide their own "safety plans." An imprisoned person voluntarily invites her loved ones, along with a prison representative, to meet in a facilitated Circle process provided by a community organization. The Circle is based on public health learning principles, and applies restorative justice and solution-focused brief therapy concepts.

The purpose of the Circle is twofold. First, the Circle process assists the incarcerated person in preparing a detailed written plan that addresses his/her needs, including reconciliation and assists them in establishing a support system for a successful return to the community. Second, the Circle provides an opportunity for loved ones to address ways that the incarcerated person may work to repair any harm they have caused to others.

The process was developed and evaluated in Hawai'i and can be replicated in any prison or confinement setting. This book describes the specific steps and provides the forms necessary for an organization to provide the process, along with suggestions for how to adapt the process to a host community's unique needs.

The book can be helpful for people working with prisons, and people harmed by crime, substance abuse, and incarceration. This book, coupled with experience working with this target population, knowledge of restorative justice principles, and exposure to solution-building brief therapy language should provide a strong foundation for recreating a similar reentry and transition planning process for any community.

The Circle process can also be provided outside of the prison setting upon an individual's release if developing a prison or institutional based program is not feasible. Circles can also be adapted and used for people transitioning out of residential substance abuse, other confinement programs, and for completing court or other supervised programs, e.g. probation, parole, etc.

---

[1] Jeremy Travis is a former director of the U.S. National Institute of Justice who has extensively researched reentry, and advocates for a public health approach.

In person training is available for organizations who would like to develop a similar program based on this process for their community, either in a prison setting or other transitional environment. In addition, a website and blog where interested individuals can post questions for the authors and share experiences with others developing a Circle process for their community is available at: http://reentrycircles.blogspot.com. For further details and training information, contact Lorenn at lorenn@hawaii.edu or lorenn@hawaii.rr.com.

Part One
A Need Addressed: Developing the Circle Process

I. Case Example

Authors' Note: The following is a case example that will be used throughout this book to illustrate the process. This example is based on actual cases from the Women's Community Correctional Center on the island of Oahu, Hawai'i with identifying information about individuals altered.

Kathy Lee

The name Lee, K., is scribbled with black felt pen over the front pocket of her blue colored hospital scrubs, the uniform for the women's prison where the 39-year-old woman has been incarcerated for the last year. Kathy Lee's hair is neatly pulled into a tight ponytail and she has on clean white running shoes. Her eyes are bright and she smiles hesitantly. Her left leg constantly jiggles as she takes quick glances at the door behind her. Kathy is sitting in a chair in a circle with a facilitator, recorder and prison counselor. The group is waiting for two of her adult children and her granddaughter to come and fill the three empty chairs in the circle. Another empty chair in the circle has sheets of paper containing information the circle facilitator obtained from Kathy's parents and her 15-year-old daughter who lives them. They live in California and could not come and personally attend the Circle.

Kathy's Huikahi Restorative Circle is being held at the prison where she expects to be released in two years. She applied for the Circle six months ago because she wants to take responsibility for repairing harm that her past behavior and her incarceration have caused her family, and for her former employer from whom she stole money. Besides addressing the need for reconciliation,[2] Kathy also wants to make a plan for meeting her other needs for a successful reentry and transition from prison back into the community. These other needs include such things as employment, housing, transportation, continued learning, and maintaining emotional and physical health.

---

[2] Please see page 42 infra for how reconciliation is defined for purposes of this reentry and transition planning process.

II. Goals and Objectives of the Circle Process

[T]he goals of a successful reentry model should be to break down the artificial construct of "us" versus "them."

- Jeremy Travis

This voluntary reentry and transition planning process brings an incarcerated adult into a facilitated meeting with his or her loved ones and a prison representative.[3] The purpose of the Circle is to give the imprisoned person an opportunity to take responsibility for her or his life by determining thier goals, identifying their strengths, and considering how they can begin to prepare to meet their needs outside of prison.[4] Needs addressed by the process include the incarcerated person's need for reconciliation and their desire to repair harm caused to loved ones. Healing for loved ones and for unrelated people who have been harmed by the imprisoned person's past behavior and imprisonment is another purpose of the Circle. While unrelated victims[5] do not participate in the Circle, the group addresses and collaborates in developing ideas for what the incarcerated person could do to make amends while still incarcerated and after release with these individuals and communities.

The people who participate in the Circle are selected entirely from a list provided by the incarcerated individual. The facilitator tries to contact everyone who the incarcerated individual would like to have participate. If physical presence is not possible, the facilitator can obtain written statements from those willing to share. Frequently, not all the individuals can participate due to scheduling and other limitations. In those cases, a Circle can proceed so long as there is one individual from the list who can be present. A prison staff person also participates. The prison representative provides valuable information for loved ones on the incarcerated person's efforts to rehabilitate in prison. Her participation also helps to improve prison culture by seeing the incarcerated person not solely as a *prisoner,* but through the eyes of the incarcerated person's

---

[3] There is also a *Modified Circle* process described infra, where loved ones do not participate, and other incarcerated people instead support the person having the Circle.

[4] The female pronouns will be used throughout for ease of description. The identical model is provided to and applicable to men and women.

[5] We make every effort to not use the terms *victim* and *offender* in this book and in providing this program. The labels are generally limiting and based on negative deficits that can create or further entrench problems. In the instances we use the terms it is only to clarify our meaning.

loved ones. After participating in the Circle and meeting the participants, the prison representative has a different, more holistic view of the incarcerated person.

The Circles are designed to increase and solidify an incarcerated person's support system in the community and family, to which she will most likely return to after release (Baer, 2006). It also provides the incarcerated person with an opportunity to develop a written transition plan outlining her goals and needs that she can realistically follow to achieve an independent life after prison. The plan also includes a timeline for any actions that she and other participants may agree to take to meet her goals and needs. The other important goal of the process is to bring healing to the people harmed by the imprisoned person's unlawful behavior and incarceration. This includes children who have suffered, and are often traumatized from their parent's criminal behavior and imprisonment (Hairston, 2007).

Follow-up Circles are planned to check the implementation of the initial plan, and to adjust for expected changes. The process is best started as close as possible to the beginning of the individual's term of imprisonment. Early provision of the process enables the incarcerated person to develop concrete ways they can make the best use of prison time, including taking advantage of any support offered from the Circle participants. In addition, the hope of reconciliation and repairing damage caused by their crimes and imprisonment can help incarcerated people with rehabilitation throughout their prison sentence.

III. History & Theory Behind the Circle Process

A. Circles in Hawai'i

The Circle process for reentry and transition planning was developed by Lorenn Walker based on a similar transition planning process she developed for foster youth emancipating from state custody (Walker, 2005). With a background as a Montessori teacher, attorney, and public health educator, Lorenn drew on her experience addressing conflicts and developing group processes. Her experience with other settings as well as a wide range of theories led to the development of this Circle process for reentry settings. In adapting this model for addressing transitions, solution-focused brief therapy language was added under the guidance of renowned therapist and co-founder of solution-focused brief therapy, the late Insoo Kim Berg.

The initial idea for this reentry and transition planning process came from John Braithwaite, Ph.D. Professor Braithwaite is an acclaimed social scientist with the Australian National University who has spent a career researching and studying strategies for peacemaking and assisting marginalized people. Braithwaite's important book *Crime, Shame and Reintegration*, published in 1989, "predicted that offenders will commit fewer repeat crimes if they feel remorse after being confronted with the harm they have caused, and are allowed to express that remorse" (The Stockholm Prize in Criminology, 2006). His book and many other works by Braithwaite make him an internationally acclaimed restorative justice expert.

In Hawai'i, the Circle process is called *Huikahi Restorative Circles*. In Hawaiian *hui* means group and *kahi* means individual, and for purposes of this process the two come together to form a mutual understanding or covenant (Walker & Greening, 2010).

The process respects each community's culture and should be adapted as such. Communities replicating it are encouraged to adopt their own unique name for the process. A New York community working to replicate the process has named it *Family Circle*.

The Huikahi Circle program was initially piloted at a men's minimum-security prison on O'ahu, and later at the Hawai'i state Women's Community Correctional Center (WCCC).[6] The program's early success motivated the Hawai'i state legislature to pass a resolution directing the state department that administers prisons to support the program statewide (Senate Concurrent Resolution 192, Senate Draft 1).

Since 2005, over 340 people, including incarcerated adults and one youth,[7] their loved ones, and prison representatives have participated in 66 Huikahi Circles.[8] Also approximately 125 incarcerated people have participated in 55 *Modified Huikahi Circles*[9] provided for members of a 12-week *solution-focused training program* for Hawai'i prisons (Walker & Sakai, 2006). Instead of loved ones attending the Modified Circles, other incarcerated participants of the solution-focused training

---

[6] WCCC is Hawai'i's only women's prison. It houses women with all levels of security assessments including low, medium and maximum. (Retrieved September 1, 2011 from: http://hawaii.gov/psd/corrections/institutions-division/prisons/womens-community-correctional-center)

[7] The first Circle for a juvenile transitioning out of the Hawai'i's youth correctional facility was successfully held on September 29, 2011.

[8] One Circle was successfully held for a Nigerian family in Helsinki, Finland for parents who are facing deportation and had been incarcerated.

[9] Some of the individuals having Modified Circles later have had a full Huikahi Circle with their loved ones and prison staff.

program played the part of supporters for the incarcerated people having the Modified Circles (Walker, 2009). One Modified Circle was provided in a Santa Cruz, California jail for an incarcerated woman. The jailed woman and three of her incarcerated friends, along with two jail staff supporters, participated in her Modified Circle.

B. Theories Behind the Process

The model is intended to incorporate a diverse set of principles from a wide range of practice areas that continually improve. In this way, the model is not merely a blueprint, but a fluid construct which remains open and responsive to new developments in the fields that it draws.

1. Public Health Learning Principals

Many respected corrections experts suggest a public health approach for the rehabilitation of imprisoned people (Zimbardo, 2008; Travis, 2005; Maruna, 2001; and Schwartz & Boodell, 2009) The World Heath Organization (WHO) has established criteria for public health educators to use in working to change human behavior (WHO, 1954).

The WHO specifies that learning is more likely to occur when there is a focus on an individual's goals; positive motivation is used; it occurs in group settings; and provides experiential, activity-based processes. These elements of an effective public health learning model are consistent with what Hans Toch, a respected American corrections expert who studies rehabilitation, says prisons should use to "improve the lives of individual inmates."

Toch argues that:

> When individuals are provided with opportunities for personal development, they will demonstrate a capacity for self-actualization. A related assumption is that change in people is best accomplished when those to be changed are engaged as partners in the change process. The third assumption has to do with the type of human organization (participatory democracy), which lends itself to active involvement and personal development (Toch, 1997, 36).

The incarcerated person drives the Circle process. It is the individual who chooses to have one and s/he who decides which loved ones and supporters to invite to attend. By embracing this opportunity for personal development, the imprisoned person increases the chances that the process will be effective in teaching them new skills and ways of thinking.

2. Restorative Justice

Restorative justice considers and works to address the needs of people hurt by crime, the people who committed the crimes, and the community (Zehr, 2002). While the modern restorative justice movement began in the 1970s, some believe that "restorative justice has been the dominant model of criminal justice throughout most of human history for perhaps all the world's peoples" (Braithwaite, 2002). Although restorative justice in Europe was largely abandoned at the time of the Norman Conquest (Van Ness, 1986), many indigenous cultures worldwide have never stopped using it (Braithwaite, 2002; Zehr, 2002). A general goal of restorative justice is to create opportunities for reconciliation between people who accept accountability for their wrongdoing and those affected by their behavior, which is not always possible. Restorative practices may be applied across a range of situations with different types of participants (Zehr, 1990; McCold & Wachtel, 2002; Walker, 2004). Restorative practices can address the unique needs of each individual including their emotional needs. These needs are largely ignored by the criminal justice system and are "subtly...suppressed, inhibited, and distorted" by prisons (Zimbardo, 2008, p. 221).

Families and friends of people who have committed crimes and are incarcerated, have been harmed by their loved one's behavior and their imprisonment. Often they suffer directly, but always they suffer indirectly. Children of incarcerated parents especially suffer hardship (Hairston, 2007). A restorative intervention, like these Circles, can provide important benefits without the participation of the unrelated crime victims.

Restorative justice approaches are evidence-based practices that have been researched and shown to reduce most types of repeat crime (Sherman & Strang, 2007). Additionally, restorative justice brings more healing to people hurt by crime than traditional court and prison practices. Today there is a growing movement to use restorative practices in reentry for incarcerated people returning to the community (Bazemore & Maruna, 2009; Walker, Sakai & Brady, 2008).

3. Solution Focused Brief Therapy

This reentry and transition planning process applies basic solution-focused brief therapy language skills. "SFBT" "SF" or "solution-building" was developed in the early 1980s by Steve de Shazer, Insoo Kim Berg, and their colleagues at the Brief Family Therapy Center in Milwaukee, Wisconsin. Berg assisted in the design of this Circle process in 2004. All Circle facilitators and recorders are trained in SFBT and apply its principles while interviewing Circle applicants; in their discussions with others convening the Circles; and in conducting Circles. Further discussion of training circle facilitators in SFBT practices is included in Part III, Section 1 of this book.

SFBT is "a competency-based model, which minimizes emphasis on past failings and problems, and instead focuses on clients' strengths and previous successes." SFBT focuses on "working from the client's understandings of her/his concern/situation and what the client might want different." (Trepper, et al., 2010, p. 8).

The basic tenants of SFBT include:
- It is based on solution-building rather than problem-solving.
- The therapeutic focus should be on the client's future goals rather than on past problems, diagnosing individuals, or current conflicts.
- Clients are encouraged to enhance and discussing useful behaviors.
- Recognizing no problem happens all the time. There are exceptions. There are times when the problem could have happened but did not. These exceptions can be used by the client and therapist to co-construct solutions.
- Therapists help clients find alternatives to current undesired patterns of behavior, cognition, and interaction that are within the clients' repertoire or can be co-constructed by therapists and clients as such.
- The model assumes that solution behaviors already exist for clients, differing from skill-building and behavior therapy interventions.
- The model asserts that small increments of change lead to large increments of change.
- The conversational skills required of the therapist to invite the client to build solutions are different from those needed to diagnose and treat client problems. (Trepper, et al., 2010).

Solution-building focuses on past successes and exceptions to problems. Identifying what we have done well in the past enables us to see our strengths and find ways to be successful again. As such, SFBT assists people "in developing a vision of a more satisfying future," and helps them develop a "deeper awareness of the strengths and resources that [they] can use in turning vision into reality" (De Jong & Berg, 2008). SFBT is optimistic in contrast to a problem-solving approach where the focus is on analyzing problems, including why and when they occur.

SFBT sees the client as the "expert in their own life." The role of counselors and therapists is more like a facilitator who empowers the client in solution building than an expert who guides their decision makng (Dejong & Berg, 2008). It is the client who "finds his or her own way to a solution based on his or her emerging definitions of goals, strategies, strengths, and resources." For situations where outside resources are necessary and appropriate to create solutions, "it is the client who takes the lead in defining the nature of those resources and how they would be useful." (Trepper et al., 2010).

SFBT accomplishes this approach through careful use of language. In this way, training and practice are critical to enable the facilitator to use SFBT effectively. These language skills are highlighted throughout this workbook, before and after sample interactions between the Circle facilitator and Circle participants are presented. SFBT language skills are particularly useful in this Circle process to help promote restorative practices. Both approaches respect each individual as competent for addressing what they need to heal from wrongdoing, and are optimistic in nature. SFBT techniques are highlighted throughout this workbook.

4. Social Psychology & Group Dynamics

The *public health learning model* articulated fifty years ago by the World Health Organization continues to be true today. Social psychology research, and what we know about how people learn, supports the public health formula for what works best to change behavior.

Kurt Lewin's work beginning in the 1930s in "group dynamics," makes clear that people are more influenced by groups than by individual thought. Lewin's experiences as a Nazi Germany refugee motivated him to study how groups influence human behavior (Hogg & Cooper, 2003). His work shows the impact of different group management approaches in influencing individual behavior.

Lewin conducted research on the effects of three different management styles: democratic, authoritarian, and laissez-faire (Lewin, et al., 1939). In a landmark study, 10 year old boys participated in each of the different types of groups with striking results. The boys in the autocratic groups were 40 times more hostile than the boys in the democratic groups. When autocratic leaders were extremely repressive, the participants acted with apathy. And the autocratic group boys were far more self-centered than the boys in the democratic groups.

The Circle is an opportunity for incarcerated people to learn how to create positive futures for themselves. By letting them figure out what they want, and how they may get what they want, they learn how to manage their lives. Incarcerated people are given information about the program and voluntarily apply for a Circle. They invite their loved ones whom they hope will want to also participate in the process. Allowing an imprisoned person the chance to take the lead in planning for his or her reentry and transition back into the community, compared to being the subject of a *case plan* prepared by professionals, is also more likely to result in increased self-efficacy [10] and learning (Bandura, 1997; Johnson & Johnson, 1994; Tharp & Gallimore, 1993).

Albert Bandura, whose work in self-efficacy concerning our beliefs about our capabilities, is renowned for his study of how people learn. Bandura showed that people learn best through experience, or *enactive learning*. The second best way people learn is by modeling and observing others. Telling people what they should do is the least effective way of learning (Bandura, 1997), yet lectures and presentations continue to be the most widely used method of education (Jarvis, 2001).

In the last ten years, "case management" has been a major innovation in corrections. Case management is a process guided by professionals. While it should include an incarcerated person's hopes, desires and goals, (Healey, 1999), the title of the process alone indicates that it is professionally managed. In contrast to case management, Circles provide enactive and modeled learning opportunities. While a facilitator manages the order of the Circle process, the focus must be on what the incarcerated person and her family want, not on what professionals think is best for them.

In sum, an incarcerated person is actively engaged in planning her/his life by participating in a Circle. S/he is envisioning what kind of life she prefers and is actively generating possibilities and alternatives to create that desired future. Circles allow the imprisoned person to be their own *case manager,* and at the same time take advantage of professionals and case managers who may attend. The Circles allow people to learn from experience. Incarcerated people directly hear and experience the emotional consequences of their past behavior and imprisonment on their loved ones. Hearing these stories can be a particularly powerful learning exercise.

---

[10] Self-efficacy is not self-esteem. "Perceived self-efficacy is concerned with judgments of personal capabilities, whereas self-esteem is concerned with judgments of self-worth" (Bandura, 1997, p. 11).

Corrections expert Hans Toch, says:

Social learning is not an intellectual exercise, but must have an unfreezing, experiential, emotional component. As a social learner you must not only understand that you keep screwing up, and see how your keep screwing up, but you must be sufficiently disgusted with yourself to stop doing what you have been doing. This process requires reliable and sustained feedback and support for change (Toch, 1997 p. 182).

The Circle is a prime opportunity for the incarcerated person to receive feedback and support for change from their loved ones, and prison staff, who participate in the process.

5. Positive Motivation & Mindfulness

The Circles use positive motivation. The Circle premise is that an incarcerated person is capable of taking responsibility to address reconciliation, and how s/he might work to make things right for her harmed family, for the community, and for herself. Thinking one can address remedies takes positive motivation.

According to Harvard psychology professor Ellen Langer who has studied mindfulness and the "power of possibility," for decades: "Every idea, person, or object is potentially simultaneously many things depending on the perspective from which it is viewed." (Langer, 1989, p. 89). Developing perspective and insight is a matter of mindfulness.

The Circle process views incarcerated people as having the capacity to mindfully manage their lives, and having the ability to address the harm that their behavior and incarceration have caused to others and to themselves. The idea of wanting to do for others, and human *generativity development,* which Erik Erikson theorized about, is something that Shadd Maruna and others have forcefully advocated for in prison settings as a key to rehabilitation and desistance from crime (Maruna, LeBel & Lanier, 2004).

Individual incarcerated people apply to have Circles. During the Circle interview they are informed that the Circle will focus on reconciliation and their goals. From the date of the interview to the actual Circle sometimes more than a year of time may pass, or the applicant could be released without ever having a Circle. Regardless, the idea that they can make plans is suggested to them which recognizes hopefulness and their ability to do things for others and themselves. When they have a Circle, a comprehensive written plan, that include timelines for taking actions with the assistance of their supporters, is prepared.

20

III. The Importance of Reentry and Transition Planning

Reentry is the process of leaving prison and returning to society. Reentry is not a form of supervision, like parole. Reentry is not a goal, like rehabilitation or reintegration. Reentry is not an option. Reentry reflects the iron law of imprisonment: they all come back.

- Jeremy Travis

A. Reentry Reality

As Jeremy Travis says in the title of his book, *But They All Come Back: Facing the Challenges of Prisoner Reentry*, most people in prison come back into our communities. Over two million people are currently imprisoned in the United States. Our communities suffer from unsustainable incarceration levels. We have dismal rehabilitation rates. Over 50% of formerly incarcerated people are back in prison within only three years after their release. Recidivism rates climb even higher thereafter (U.S. Bureau of Justice Statistics, 2002). In Hawai'i, over 60% of those released from state prisons without supervision (probation or parole) re-offend, on average, within 12 months of their release (Interagency Council on Intermediate Sanctions, State of Hawai'i, 2010).

Especially troubling is that over 90%, of those convicted and sentenced for felonies, plead guilty to criminal charges (Hall, 2011). Yet our current system does not encourage accountability. Sentencing processes do not ask people pleading guilt to address how their behavior affected others, or ask defendants what they could possibly do to repair the harm they caused. This is true even when almost 50% of violent crimes are committed between people who know each other (Federal Bureau of Investigation, 2003).

Besides overlooking accountability, our criminal justice system also largely ignores the needs of those hurt by crime, who are often the perpetrator's loved ones. This reentry and transition group planning process gives incarcerated people and their loved ones an opportunity to address their need to heal and rebuild their lives, beginning with reconciliation.

"Reentry is a time, if managed correctly, when networks can be enhanced, collective capacities augmented, and reentering residents helped to improve the locations where they live rather than further drain them." (Rose & Clear, 2002). One man who had a Circle said, "I want to move back to my old neighborhood. I helped wreck the place, and I wanna go back and help fix it back up. It's the least I can do." Five years after the man made that statement he has remained law abiding, clean and sober, employed, and financially independent.

While life is unpredictable, one thing we can always predict is change. Life is never permanent. No matter how uncomfortable, changes happen. Birth, childhood, adolescence, maturity, old age, and death happen to everyone. Our individual needs including housing, employment, schools, and social support, change throughout our lives. Addressing and managing change with preparation and planning can result in smoother transitions. While most of us can often control and prepare for when and how we will manage our major life changes, people like Kathy discussed in this book, will eventually leave prison often lacking the opportunity for preparation, and without skills to successfully manage life back in the community.

Unfortunately the criminal justice system is paternal in nature (Mills, 1998), and prisons create a paternalistic environment by providing for the most basic needs and exerting extreme control over inmates. For people transitioning from prison, preparing and planning for that major change, and assuming responsibility to meet their own needs, is especially vital. To make a successful transition from prison an incarcerated person must find ways to reengage in the community and take responsibility for their needs. If we expect people coming out of prison to be independent and crime free, we need to ensure they are provided with the opportunity to prepare for and to practice being independent. For formerly incarcerated people to be responsible, policy makers and prison systems likewise must be responsible, and give the incarcerated opportunities to prepare for their reentry.

Prisons often provide extended institutional programs where people can practice being independent. Work or educational "furlough programs" are normally for people on parole or probation, where they can work or go to school outside of prison, but come back to the facility at night to sleep. The programs are an opportunity to practice taking responsibility before completely assuming it. When people are on parole or probation, and not in furlough programs, they have a person assigned who supervises their activities and can be a resource. This period of parole or probation can be a trial period of taking responsibility with support.

Parole, probation and work furlough programs do not apply to a large percentage of people leaving prison after serving their entire sentences. People not allowed probation, parole or furlough programs are normally sentenced for the most serious crimes and are deemed uncooperative in prison. A term commonly used by correctional facilities for this group of people is "max out," which means they will serve the maximum term imposed by the court when they were sentenced, without parole or work furlough at the end of their sentence. The people who max out, eventually return to the community, and they especially need assistance in reentry and transition planning.

Prison systems that ignore the reentry and transitional needs of incarcerated people convicted for the most serious crimes and/or who behave badly in prison, put their communities at risk for increased crime. Statistics are clear that people who exit prison without being in any extended program are more at risk for repeat crime, and more serious crimes (Interagency Council on Intermediate Sanctions, 2010). Circles could be provided for people who are going to max out, resulting in safer communities.

B. The Impact of the Correctional Approach to Substance Abuse

Law and order exist for the purpose of establishing justice and when they fail in this purpose they become the dangerously structured dams that block the flow of social progress.
- Rev. Dr. Martin Luther King Jr.

A serious problem of correctional institutions is that most of them have "zero tolerance" for substance abuse, when over half of the incarcerated people have addiction problems. Carole Dweck, and others who study how people learn, have established the importance of making mistakes for learning. Experiencing failure is natural and necessary for learning.

Basketball legend Michael Jordan affirms the importance of making mistakes and failure: "I have missed more than 9,000 shots in my career. I have lost almost 300 games. On 26 occasions I have been entrusted to take the game winning shot . . . and I missed. And I have failed over and over and over again in my life. And that is precisely why I succeed (Jordan, 2011).

Unless we accept that setbacks, failure and mistakes will happen, without challenging and blaming our innate ability to learn, we will not learn as much as we could (Dweck, 2006).

No one knows how to ride a bike instantly. No one is so "gifted" they learned everything without effort and practice. We learn from practice and unless we give people the opportunity to practice, and make mistakes, they are less likely to learn. The idea of zero tolerance contradicts the concept that people learn through their mistakes. Treating substance abuse with absolute zero tolerance, and imposing prison instead of rehabilitative programs is especially harmful.

An example of the impact of such polices is illustrative. A man about 35 years old was in a prison furlough program that had zero tolerance for substance abuse. He had a history of being in and out of prison and drug treatment programs for about 20 years. After his last prison release the man was placed into a work furlough program with zero tolerance and any infraction of the rules against drinking or taking drugs, would send him directly back into prison. A short time into the program, he broke the rules and drank alcohol before he returned to the facility for the night. The person responsible for checking him in noticed he smelled of alcohol and spoke to him about his drinking. The man was remorseful and sorry, but he assumed he would be sent back to prison as he had been the other times he relapsed while in furlough programs. He was hugely surprised when the person checking him in that night said, "I'm not telling anyone. I'm giving you another chance. I believe you regret your mistake and you won't do it again." The man was stunned, and since that night, about two years later, he had remained clean and sober. He said he had maintained sobriety since that night because: "I never got a second chance before. The guy trusted me."[11] Relapses are mistakes and should be considered learning opportunities. Correctional programs do not enhance public safety, or further rehabilitation, by imposing zero tolerance for substance abuse relapses.

C. Circles Promote Criminal Desistance from Criminal Activity

Criminal rehabilitation research shows that most people eventually outgrow their bad behavior (Maruna, 2006). "The phenomenon of natural desistance" (Rumgay, 2004) describes how people who engage in criminal behavior are able to stay crime free after deciding to reform (Maruna, 2001). Shadd Maruna has spent a career studying criminal desistance. His book *Making Good: How Ex-Convicts Reform and Rebuild Their Lives*, first published in 2001, is considered a "masterpiece" by many including Martine Herzog-Evans, a French criminal justice professor and author of numerous criminal justice books and articles.

Maruna advises it is more important to focus on how people manage to stay crime free, rather than focusing on why they decide to stop committing crimes. He points to overwhelming

---

[11] The man told this story with some advocates for the program present who made Lorenn promise to never identify what program he was in, or even what country it occurred. They were afraid that the program would be punished, and possibly shut down, if anyone learned that "zero tolerance" was not applied when the man relapsed.

evidence and agreement in the "research community" that eventually "the vast majority of delinquents and adult offenders reliably desist from offending behavior in later life (Rutherford, 1992)" (Maruna, 2001, p. 20). Desistance is an ongoing process and "sustained desistance most likely requires a fundamental and intentional shift in a person's sense of self" (Maruna, 2001, p. 17).

This finding is consistent with what Cy Kalama, a longtime Hawai'i prison drug treatment counselor who has participated in numerous prison Circles, who says: "the Circles are a place to say who the new man is, who the new warrior is, compared to the old man and the old slave they used to be . . . Circles are a place to express hopes and dreams and find what's needed specifically for a good life. They help create a support network." (Walker, 2009, p. 427).

Maruna's believes "that to successfully maintain abstinence from crime, ex-offenders need to make sense of their lives. This sense-making commonly takes the form of a life story or self-narrative" (Maruna, 2006). The Circles are an opportunity for incarcerated people to tell a new story about themselves. A story where they are accountable for their lives, including working to repair any harm they caused their loved ones, others, and themselves. The Circles encourage individuals to explain how they have transformed. Many opportunities arise during the Circle to discuss their transformation, including when they are asked: "What were you thinking back then when the crime was committed? What do you think now looking back on how you thought then?"

The Circles also focus on what the person likes and wants to do with their life, and other vital needs including how they will find work and who their supporters are. These needs have been identified as factors that promote criminal desistance. Research shows that people most commonly desist from criminal behavior when they find meaningful work, and are in relationships with law abiding members of society (Shover, 1996).

D. Circles Promote Growth Mindsets

Carol Dweck has studied motivation and learning for many years. She states, "failure can be a painful experience. But it doesn't have to define you. It's a problem to be faced, dealt with, and learned from" (Dweck, 2006, p. 33). "Dweck's research is heartening because it suggests that at all ages, people can learn to see mistakes not as terrible personal failings to be denied or justified, but as inevitable aspects of life that help us grow and grow up" (Tavris & Aronson, 2007, p. 235).

The Circles help people learn to have a "growth mindset," which "is based on the belief that your basic qualities are things you can cultivate through your efforts. Although people may differ in every which way—in their initial talents and aptitudes, interests, or temperaments—everyone can change and grow through application and experience." Growth mindsets lead to significantly higher achievement levels and to happier lives, compared to "fixed mindsets" that are based on the belief that "your qualities are carved in stone" (Dweck, 2006 p. 6 - 7).

Part Two
A Detailed Description of the
Reentry & Transition Planning Group Process

The following is a detailed description of the full reentry and transition planning process for prisons.[12]

<u>Summary of the Steps in the Process</u>

Step 1: Introduction of Reentry & Transition Planning Circle Program at Prisons

Step 2: Application for Circle Process

Step 3: Solution-Focused Interview of Circle Applicants

Step 4: Convening the Circle

Step 5: Conducting the Circle

Step 6: Circle Summary and Transition Plan Preparation and Delivery to Participants

Step 1: Introduction of Reentry & Transition Planning Circle Program at Prisons

The process is introduced at a prison by providing information and seeking incarcerated applicants to participate voluntarily.[13] It was introduced at Hawai'i's women's prison by posting one-page flyers around the facility announcing a presentation about the program. Two facilitators from the non-profit organization providing the program went into the prison to explain the Circle process. A one-hour presentation including testimonials by several women who had Modified Circles earlier, a question and answer period, a brochure explaining the process, and a one-page application form

---

[12] While the process has been mainly piloted in adult prisons, it can be used for both adults and youth transitioning out of other institutions including residential substance abuse treatment programs, etc..

[13] Alternatively, the process could be mandated by court, through statute, or as a program requirement for prison programs. Incarcerated people could be required to apply for Circles and if after an interview about it they did not want one, they could discontinue the program. Chances are many would want to participate in Circles once understanding more about the process and they could benefit from the solution-focused interview regardless of ever having a Circle.

for interested incarcerated women, was provided. A prison-staff liaison was also present.

The Circle application form and the brochure are included in Appendix A & B respectively. The brochure, "What to Expect at a Circle," explains the Circle process and states that the two main purposes of the program are to:

1. Provide people harmed by an imprisoned person's crimes and incarceration the opportunity to address what they need to heal; and

2. Provide the imprisoned person with the opportunity to find ways to make amends with loved ones and unrelated crime victims, and to meet their other essential needs for a positive life.

Step 2: Application for Circle Process

After the program is introduced at a prison, incarcerated individuals apply for a Circle. A simple one-page application is provided to the prison liaison who distributes them to the women (Appendix A). When the liaison receives a filled out application, she reviews it, and if acceptable,[14] transmits it to the sponsoring organization, which schedules a time to interview the applicant in prison.

Step 3: Solution-Focused Interview of Circle Applicants

After the community provider receives the application, usually by fax, the assigned facilitator arranges to interview the incarcerated person in the prison through the prison liaison. The personal interview takes about thirty minutes, but time permitting, an interview can take an hour or more. The facilitator who will be convening and conducting the Circle, and who will also prepare the written Circle summary and transition plan that results from the Circle, interviews the applicant.

The purpose of the interview is to ensure the applicant understands the nature of the Circle, which is to make amends with loved ones, and to make a plan for reentry back into the community.

---

[14]

Because the applicants are in state custody, the initial determination on appropriateness of a Circle for individual incarcerated people falls first to the prison. The criteria for the organization providing the Circles is that the person takes responsibility for their future and wants to make amends for any harm caused to others by their past behavior and incarceration. Whether these criteria are met is determined at a personal interview. To date, all 150 people who have applied for Circles in Hawai'i have met these criteria.

Another goal of the interview is to increase the incarcerated person's confidence and their understanding that their efforts make a difference, and their behavior affects their futures. The objective is to help her recognize that she has succeeded in achieving goals in the past despite her current imprisonment. Having hope is important for incarcerated people to successfully transition back into the community (Howerton, et. al., 2009). Optimism is vital for health and happiness (Brantley, 2007; Seligman, 2006).

During the interview the facilitator reviews the information on the one page application. Age, education, anticipated prison release date, charges currently being held in prison for, a list of people who were harmed by prior criminal behavior and incarceration, and the names of others who support them, including counselors and other professionals, are on the application. During the interview the facilitator also tells the incarcerated person that at least one person not in prison must agree to come to her Circle in order to conduct one. Applicants are also told if they are not provided a Circle while they are in prison, they could have one after their release. Out of the 66 Circles provided to date, four were held outside of prison after the incarcerated applicants were released.

TECHNIQUE HIGHLIGHT: IDENTIFYING STRENGTHS & MAKING COMPLIMENTS

The solution-focused language used in the interview is designed to gather information about the incarcerated person's successes, competencies, and strengths, however small, and to provide information on what to expect at the Circle (Lee, Sebold & Uken, 2003). The anecdotal evidence of the hopefulness generated from Circles is apparent from the people who have been interviewed. Typically people come to the interviews with depressed demeanors, their heads down, little eye contact shared, and they are generally nervous and anxious. As the interview progresses their faces brighten, postures straighten, eye contact and smiles are shared more, and they engage more enthusiastically. The facilitator compliments them on their strengths (De Jong & Berg, 2008). Compliments validate what people are already doing well, which combined with acknowledging how difficult their problems are, encourages people to change while giving them the message that the facilitator has been listening, understands, and cares about them (Trapper, et al., 2010).

A. The Interview

Interview with Applicant Kathy (K) & the Circle facilitator (F)

F: [Facilitator looks Kathy in the eye, smiling and extends her hand for a friendly handshake] "Glad to meet you Kathy. My name is Donna and I came to see you about your application for a Huikahi Circle."

K: [tentatively smiling] "Hi."

F: "It's so great to meet someone who takes responsibility for herself and wants a Circle to make a plan for the future and make things right with their family."

K: [more broadly smiling] "Thanks. Nice to meet you."

F: "You look so fit and healthy. How have you managed to do that in here?"

K: "Oh, I walk as much as I can and do exercises everyday. I work in the kitchen too. I do as much as I can to keep busy."

F: "That's great! You're exercising everyday, working in the kitchen and keeping busy. How do you manage to do all that?"

K: "Oh, I've always worked, no matter what. I've worked since I was 15."

F: "Wow! you've been a hard worker most of your life! What does that say about you that you're such a hard worker since you were only 15 Kathy?"

K: "I dunno, we had no money. I had to work or I wouldn't have anything. My grandma worked hard and my mom, we all work.

F: "What would your Grandma and mom say about you if they could see how hard you are working to make things better?"

K: "One thing they know about me is that I am a hard worker."

F: "And you keep working even in prison. You could just be lying around here. I know they don't make you work. What does it say about you that you chose to work?"

K: "Hummm....I guess that I don't give up. Jus cuz I'm in prison doesn't mean, I'm gonna quit working hard and trying to make things better."

F: "Good for you working so hard and trying to make things better Kathy. What makes you want to have a Circle?"

K: "I hurt so many people. I want to make amends and show my girls how sorry I am for what I did. I was stupid. I don't want 'em to make the same mistakes."

F: "What a good mom you are. Wanting to make amends and show your girls how sorry you are. You're making something positive out of the mistakes you made by teaching them something. You could be all bummed out, feeling sorry for yourself about being in prison, but instead here your are, working hard, and doing things to help your girls. That's inspiring."

(cont.)

K: [brightly smiling] "Thanks. My girls mean more to me than anything. I tried to always do the right thing and got involved with the wrong guy, their dad. He's in federal prison. He's been my downfall. I don't hate him and I know it was my decision to stay with him, but I will never be with him again."

F: "Wow, you put your girls first, and know you should do the right thing. You saw their dad was a negative influence on you and you've changed that. That must have been hard. He must have meant a lot to you. How'd you do that? How'd you get out of a relationship with him?

K: "When I got arrested and knew my girls would be without me, I knew right then I had to decide who meant more to me, and I picked my girls. They are good kids and their dad's a loser. He's all about himself. He don't work, and I am over trying to help him clean up his act. He's not worth it. I was to be there for my girls."

F: "Good for you Kathy. Sounds like you're on the right track, wanting to be there for your girls. Having the Circle can help. Here is some information about the Circle for you."

[Facilitator pulls out a one-page brochure, showing it to Kathy]

F: "First we'll all be sitting in a circle of chairs somewhere here at the prison. Of all the people you listed on your application, who do you want to sit right next to you in the Circle?"

K: "Shelly, she's the youngest, and it's been hardest on her."

F: "Okay. After everyone comes and signs in, I'll ask you to "open" the Circle. Basically that's anything symbolic you want to say or do. You can sing a song, say a prayer, ask one of the participants to, or you can read a statement you wrote earlier, or recite a poem, whatever you want to open the process, okay?"

The facilitator goes on to explain the steps in the process,
circling the points in the brochure they are reviewing that Kathy needs to prepare for.

F: "At the Circle I'll ask you what you're most proud of having accomplished since you've been here in prison. What would you say?"

K: "I guess just learning about myself. Doing a lot of work on myself to see where I went wrong. I been taking a parenting course where I'm learning to be open about my feelings and just about being a better person besides being a better mom."

F: [extending her hand and a warm pat on Kathy's upper arm] "It was really special meeting you Kathy. Thank you for sharing your good ideas and your hopes for you and your girls. I hope you'll keep doing what you're doing here, taking classes, looking for ways to learn more about yourself and staying connected to your family. If you have any more questions or anything please phone or write us a letter. We gave stamps to the prison so you can write us for free. If you don't hear from us about your Circle, please contact us. If you don't get a Circle while you're in here, call us when you get out. We do them on the outside; actually it's a lot easier that way. Keep up your hard work in here to do better Kathy, and I look forward to meeting your daughters."

B. Commentary on Interview

One vital aspect of SF is doing *surface assessments* of incarcerated people and not engaging in any chronological or historical studies about people. "Effective solution-focused assessment requires the facilitator to stay on the surface, avoiding any 'deep' assumptions about why people are behaving as they are at a given moment and instead focusing on the value of any given presentation" (Lee, Sebold & Uken, 2003 p. 25). Circle facilitators do not seek any details about what crimes were committed. The SF approach recognizes that this type of information subtly biases people in negative ways. Therefore the interview does not delve into what brought the individual to prison or their prior bad acts. Instead the facilitator focuses on accomplishments.

Every incarcerated person has had a positive response when asked about his or her accomplishments. The question helps people see that they have achieved positive outcomes, regardless of being in prison and their past misbehavior. Many identify the positive things they have learned about themselves while imprisoned. The facilitator's statements to Kathy, *co-constructed* her version of Kathy's situation.

The facilitator's statements were a formulation that grounded Kathy into accepting her strengths (Sacks & Garfinkel, 1970). The facilitator said that it was "great to meet someone taking responsibility" for herself by applying for a Circle. These words formulated the facilitator's interpretation of Kathy's wish to have a Circle. Kathy grounded by immediately providing information about herself consistent with the facilitator's formulation, thus accepting the positive way of looking at her behavior. Grounding naturally occurs in all human dialogues.

> [G]rounding is a collaborative process in which both participants are responsible for ensuring that they understand each other. Because each grounding cycle potentially creates new common ground, the speaker and addressee are continuously co-constructing a shared version of events. . . Grounding is a sequential process that occurs constantly, moment-by-moment, as a speaker presents some information, the other person confirms that he or she understood it (or not), and the speaker indicates, implicitly or explicitly, that the other person has understood correctly (or not) (Clark,1996; Dejong, et al, in press).

During the interview, the facilitator offered a positive version of Kathy's situation, which she accepted and it became common ground in the dialogue. Research on the application of solution-focused language compared to cognitive behavioral therapy, shows that the solution-focused approach results in more positive grounding (Smock, et al, 2010).

The interview also ends positively often with a suggestion of something to work on to continue learning. The idea of homework is part of a solution-focused discussion. Leaving the incarcerated person with something to work on after the interview, gives them something tangible to continue in the future. It provides them with further hope, and a clear message that what they do influences their life.

In addition to using SF language to ground Kathy positively, the non-verbal cues are also likely to be a positive influence. According to Ellen Langer, "We react to silence, tone of voice, and nonverbal cues even if we are not aware of it." When the facilitator kindly touched Kathy the cue is that she is one of us and not a horrible person because she is imprisoned and committed crimes. Humanizing people is necessary for rehabilitating incarcerated populations. Many prisons admonish people working in them to "not touch prisoners," which sadly contributes to the mentality of "them and us," and hampers rehabilitation.

Requiring that people wear uniforms, calling people *inmates* and by numbers, not their names, and yelling at them, leads to dehumanization. Philip Zimbardo, principal researcher of the historic and remarkable 1971 *Stanford Prison Experiment* has extensively studied the effects of dehumanization on incarcerated people and their jailors. He says:

> Dehumanization occurs whenever some human beings consider other human beings to be excluded from the moral order of being a human person. The objects of this psychological process lose their human status in the eyes of their dehumanizers. By identifying certain individuals or groups as being outside the sphere of humanity, dehumanizing agents suspend the morality that might typically govern reasoned actions toward their fellows (Zimbardo, 2008 p. 307).

Circle facilitators are aware of the subtle ways the interview process can be a humanizing rather than a dehumanizing experience.

The importance of the interview phase is underscored by the realities of limited program resources. In Hawai'i, the program is funded with small private grants and pro bono efforts. Not all who apply and are interviewed can be provided a Circle. Priority goes to people being discharged from prison soonest, or those facing other pressing family problems. Even if an incarcerated person only receives an interview as a result of the program, there are positive benefits because the solution-focused interview engages the incarcerated person in a hopeful dialogue, emphasizing their strengths, and their ability to create a positive future (Walker, 2008).

Step 4: Convening the Circle

A. Reaching Out

After interviewing the imprisoned applicant, the time consuming task of arranging the Circle begins. Convening the Circle includes calling all the people the applicant listed on her application; explaining the process to them; describing what to expect and what will be discussed at a Circle; how it can be emotional to participate; asking if they want to attend; and finding a date and time that will work for all the people willing to come and the prison. These arrangements, which are made by the facilitator, take an average ten hours of time. Five people are the average number of participants at most Circles.

Most people are interested in the Circle invitation and want more information, including how long the Circle takes, and when it would be scheduled. Depending on the prison administration, and how receptive it is to the program, the Circles are arranged around the invitees' schedules. Flexible prison administrators have allowed Circles on weekends and evenings to accommodate working families.

> **Initial telephone call to an invited loved one:**
>
> "Hi, this is Donna Smith, with Hawai'i Friends of Justice & Civic Education. Kathy Lee gave me your number. I work with the Huikahi Circle prison program. It's only for people in prison who take responsibility for their behavior and imprisonment. They want to make amends with their family and other people they've hurt and make a plan for a positive future. It's also a chance for the family to say what it's been like for them, and what the person in prison might do to make things right. Kathy's applied for a Circle and hopes you would want to attend. Does this sound like something you might be interested in?"

Some loved ones are unable to come to prisons for Circles. Reasons include that their inability to take time off work, they have children to care for, are ill, have criminal records themselves and aren't allowed to visit prisons, or live too far away. Most incarcerated people in Hawai'i, as well as the rest of the United States, come from families who are struggling financially, and many do not live near the prisons. The program tries to have some transportation funds to help pay at least half the airfare for those who need it to travel to O'ahu from neighboring islands. In one case the program helped pay the fare from the continental United States. Additionally, the prisons where the program has been piloted on O'ahu are located in rural areas off direct bus routes. The program providers have arranged to pick people up from bus stops, the airport, or close to their homes on O'ahu so they can attend Circles.

A small percentage of people have said, "No," they are not interested in participating a Circle during the five years the program has been piloted in Hawai'i. It is understandable that some family members are estranged from imprisoned loved ones. When they say they do not want to participate, the facilitator typically says something like:

> "Of course you know what's best for you and your family. Please know though this program is as much for you as it is for Kathy. You've been affected by her behavior and imprisonment and it's a chance for you to explain that to her. May I send you a brochure in the mail with more information about the Circles, and if you'd like, we could talk about it again after you look at it?"

Most people want the brochure. Some who initially said they did not want to attend changed their minds after reading the brochure and further discussion. To date everyone who has participated in Circles, reports satisfaction with the process (Walker & Greening, 2010).

It is important to note that when an incarcerated person requests the presence of a minor at the Circle, facilitators cannot speak directly to the minors without the consent of their guardians. It is left up to the parents and guardians whether or not to bring a minor to a Circle. The facilitators tell caretakers that the experience of children has been successful at Circles.

Infants and children of all ages have successfully attended Circles. Three-year-old children have sat in Circles without problems. Sometimes an observer will be watching a Circle and draw or play with young children attending, but all children to date have successfully attended Circles.

B. When Invited Participants Cannot be Physically Present

For the loved ones who would attend Circles if they could, but cannot, an opportunity for them to participate is provided. Unfortunately, the use of speaker phones for participants who cannot be present is not currently an option for Hawai'i prisons. If a prison did allow speakerphones they could be used during a Circle to connect family unable to attend.

An alternative to active telephonic participation for loved ones unable to physically attend, is a solution-focused telephonic interview by the facilitator who collects their information before the Circle. The statements made during the interview are printed, left in an empty chair during the CIrcle, and read at the appropriate time by a loved one in attendance. Some of these interviews by phone can last over an hour. For most people it is the first time anyone has asked them how they were affected by their loved one's criminal behavior and incarceration, and what might be done to repair the harm.

Portion of an Interview with Participant who Cannot be Physically Present

F: "How were you affected by Kathy's prior behavior and her imprisonment?"

KM: "It's been hard. We're grandparents and have been raising one of her daughters for 2 years. We should be spoiling her and instead we have to discipline. I never talk negative about her parents, but it's been hard. It's hard financially and it's hard physically. We have a small income, and we're in our 60s."

F: "That's so commendable. It's been hard for you but you've put your granddaughter before yourselves. How have you managed to do that?"

KM: "When my daughter went to prison there was no way I would have my granddaughter go into foster care. The other girls were older and could take care of themselves, but this little one needed us. That's what family is for, to help when you need it. My grand kids are all good kids. And the one we've been raising is doing great. She gets good grades, does sports and stays away from the bad crowd."

F: "What a good job you've been doing raising her. She gets good grades and does sports and has learned to stay away from the bad crowd. And you're teaching all your grandchildren what family means."

Later in the conversation Kathy\s mother explains
what she would like Kathy to do to help with the hardship.

F: "What could Kathy possibly to do help repair some of the harm Mrs. Lee?"

KM: "She can get herself together and be the mom she is supposed to be."

F: "What do you mean exactly 'get herself together'?"

KM: "She can get a job when she gets out and keep it. And get her daughter back and take care of her."

For Kathy's family, and the loved ones of other incarcerated people living outside Hawai'i or on neighbor islands, gaining their input for the Circles has been a vital part of the process. After five years the program began collecting qualitative data on the importance of the interviews for those who could not attend. The family members consistently state that although they could not be present, the conversations with the facilitator helped them. For many it was the first time anyone asked how things have been for them at all. The justice system usually does not focus on the effects of crime on people unless it is relevant to proving guilt or imposing sentences. How criminal behavior and incarceration affect families is overlooked. This disregard communicates to families that their voice and pain are unimportant and not valued.

The importance of the facilitator interviewing Kathy's mother is evident. Mrs. Lee said afterwards that her conversation with the facilitator was beneficial because: "It helped me by making me stronger, knowing somebody is out there to help her [Kathy]. That there is someone who cares [about Kathy] and who she can talk to." Kathy's 15-year-old daughter, who Kathy's mother cares for was also unable to attend the Circle. She said the phone interview helped her: "To be able to tell my mom how I am feeling, takes it out, makes me feel better."

Step 5: Conducting the Circle

Summary of The Circle Process

1. Circle Opening
2. Proudest Accomplishments in Prison
3. Identifying Strengths
4. Addressing Reconciliation Needs
5. Break
6. Specifying Goals
7. Making Plans for Meeting Practical Needs
8. Setting the Re-Circle Date
9. Closing Circle
10. Surveys and Data Collection
11. Breaking of Bread

Introduction & Set-up

The facilitator who convenes the Circle conducts it along with a trained recorder. The recorder will collect all the important information the group provides on large sheets of paper posted on walls, which will be given to the facilitator after the Circle for inclusion in the written Circle Summary and Transition Plan.

The room is arranged with a circle of chairs, with the recorder standing outside the Circle writing with bright felt pens on the paper as people speak. An agenda of the process is printed on a large sheet of paper for the group to see during the process so everyone knows exactly what points will be covered, and when they will be addressed. See Appendix D for a sample facilitator's agenda.

Before the process begins a sign in sheet is distributed for people to sign that includes a confidentiality provision. Children are also asked to sign in, to respect and validate their participation. See Appendix E for a sign in sheet example.

The facilitator takes a blank copy of the Circle Summary with spaces large enough to write notes in by hand during the process. (Appendix C). The facilitator's notes on the blank Circle Summary form will be used, along with the recorder's large sheets of paper, to construct a the final written Circle Summary and Transition plan which is mailed to each household with attending members. For example, Kathy's two daughters who attended her Circle will receive one copy of the Summary at their shared household. Kathy's friend Liz who attended will receive a copy, and Kathy's mother and 15-year-old daughter, who were interviewed by telephone, will receive a copy mailed to their home in California. Earl who participated on behalf of the prison will also receive a copy of the Summary. See Appendix G for the Circle Summary and Transition plan for the example of Kathy Lee.

1. Circle Opening

The Circle begins with the incarcerated person opening it in any way she chooses. This is one of the points she is prepared for during the initial interview. Circles have been opened with songs, playing a guitar or ukulele, prayers, poems, reading a written statement, giving a native Hawaiian chant, or asking someone else in the Circle to say a prayer, or something that sets a positive tone for reconciliation.

2. The Incarcerated Person's Proudest Accomplishments in Prison

After the Circle opening, and all the participants have introduced themselves, the incarcerated person describes her proudest accomplishments since she has been in prison. The list of accomplishments shows attending family members early in the process the positive things the incarcerated person has been doing in prison. This helps provide positive examples to the family instead of reinforcing the negative blaming and complaining that people tend to engage in when a family member has been incarcerated. This type of negative talk can lead to more dissension and problems. Beginning in a positive fashion sets the tone for the remainder of the Circle. For family who cannot attend, as in Kathy's case, they can read about the accomplishments that will be included in the Circle Summary and Transition Plan that is sent to them after the Circle.

Addressing the Incarcerated Person's Accomplishments

K: "I got my GED. I finished the drug treatment program up here. I took parenting and anger management."

F: "That's great! You really made the most of your time in prison. How did you do all that?"

K: "I just did it. I want to come out of here better and I am gonna do it. I am sick and tired of feeling sick and tired."

F: "Wow, you're sick and tired of feeling sick and tired! And you're willing to do the work it takes to make a better life for yourself. Is there anything else you are especially proud of accomplishing in prison?"

K: "Oh yeah, I quit smoking two years ago now."

F: "That must have been really hard. How'd you do that?"

K: "I just went through it. I drank a lot of water and did other stuff, like get up and walk when I wanted a smoke. That craving went away finally. I am never going back to it." ....

F: "Kathy you have a lot of self-discipline to deal with craving. It's really impressive.
On a scale of 0 to 10 with 0 being you will go back to smoking and 10 being you for sure won't go back, where are you honestly as you sit here today on that scale?"

K: "I'm a 10. I will never pick up another ciggy!"

F: "Wow that's great! What makes you so sure you "will never pick one up again?"

K: "I feel so much better. No more hacking every morning. Feeling like I was gonna die gasping for breath when I walked up stairs. Plus it was really hard to kick. I am never going back."

F: "OK, so what would it take to make you even more sure of yourself, like make you are a 10.5 on the scale?"

K: "I just need to keep doing what I've been doing. Working out. Using my breath for good things, and for sure for not using. I think staying clean keeps me away from wantin to smoke. It's all drugs."

F: "You have a lot of insight into yourself Kathy. Seeing how working out, staying clean keeps you wanting to stay healthy, that cigarettes are drugs too. You have good ideas. What does it tell you about yourself that you did all this work, you had the perseverance to get your GED, finish the drug treatment program, and take parenting and anger management?"

K: "I love my family and want to be a better mom and daughter. I want to be a mother to my children and take care of them, not be a problem for them or my mother."

SFBT TECHNIQUE HIGHLIGHT: SCALING QUESTIONS & SELF-COMPLIMENTS

One of the more beneficial SFBT skills employed by a facilitator is the use of scaling questions. These are questions that the facilitator asks when the incarcerated individual identifies a specific goal or objective. The use of a scaling question allows the individual to make a self-assessment and evaluate their own progress. Based on the named goal or objective, the facilitator will ask the incarcerated individual to place themselves on a scale from 1 - 10 (or 0 - 10), 1 representing the worst possible scenario / no change and 10 representing achievement of the goal or ideal situation. "Within this framework it is possible to define ultimate objectives, what the client is already doing to achieve them, and what the next step might be" (Iverson, 2002).

Once a person "places" themselves on the scale, the facilitator can comment on their number exploring the decision to choose that number. Highlighting small, positive changes that can be made to move "up" the scale is also possible by the facilitator asking how the incarcerated individual can do to move even half of a point "up" the scale. In addition, if a follow-up Circle occurs, the facilitator can ask the question again to measure progress or address difficulties.

This tool is also useful as a communication device between the incarcerated individual and other circle participants. For example, if the incarcerated individual scales their confidence they will be able to achieve a named goal, the facilitator can ask the incarcerated individual to explain why they placed themselves where they did on the scale. Useful questions to ask include: "What do you know about yourself that your [name of present family member] doesn't know about you?" This gives the incarcerated individual a chance to explain positive changes they have made and what steps they have already taken towards achieving their goals. In addition, the facilitator can use this as an opportunity to elicit a self-compliment by asking the incarcerated individual: "What does it say about you that you were able to accomplish this?" Self-compliments are a powerful SFBT tool as individuals are called upon to see and name their own positive characteristics and strengths.

3. Identifying Strengths

After discussing what the incarcerated person has achieved in prison, her strengths, or "what people like about her," are identified next. If any children or young adults attend the Circle, their strengths are also identified as strengths for the incarcerated person. The group lists each young person's strengths, which is a moving experience for everyone. We do not often take time to discuss in groups what we like about people. For children, who are more often corrected for misbehavior, to hear what their families like about them, is a rare and wonderful experience for everyone in the Circles.

Next, each person identifies the incarcerated person's additional strengths. It can be a very emotional time for the incarcerated person since this may be the first time a group has ever acknowledged her positive attributes. Many become tearful, including loved ones, prison staff and even the facilitator and recorder. Tissues are always provided at the Circles. After everyone in the Circle says what he or she likes about the incarcerated person, she is asked, "What other strengths do you have that were not mentioned here?" Usually, they say "That's all," but occasionally someone will offer such as, "I'm pretty funny."

SFBT TECHNIQUE HIGHLIGHT: COPING & REFRAMING FOR STRENGTHS

It is not uncommon for an individual to not be able to identify their own strengths while facing a difficult situation where they feel hopeless. It is hard for them to imagine things being different or to find value in their present situation of incarceration. In these situations it is useful for the facilitator to delve into how the incarcerated individual has managed to cope despite their feelings of hopelessness (Iverson, 2002). In addition, it is useful to "reframe" perceived weaknesses or difficulties into strengths, e.g. "I am stubborn," reframed into "You are determined." Once the incarcerated individual is able to describe ways they have coped in the past, the facilitator can again compliment them on their abilities, or solicit a self-compliment by asking them to say what their ability to cope tells everyone about them.

It is important to note that both the facilitator and recorder are careful to use the exact words spoken by participants when repeating or reframing things they say. Using the precise words used by participants is respectful and an important feature of solution-focused language skills.

4. Addressing Reconciliation Needs

A. The Unique Needs of Incarcerated People

The Circles address the practical needs an incarcerated person has for a successful transition and reentry back into the community. For people coming out of prison, there is a need for reconciliation. While many consider reconciliation to be synonymous with restoration, which is the ultimate hope for restorative justice programs, reconciliation can mean something less. It can simply mean *the process of making consistent or compatible.*

Loved ones who attend Circles have the need to address any pain they suffered by the incarcerated person's criminal behavior and imprisonment. Children especially benefit from discussing how the imprisonment of a parent has affected them. The Circles allow incarcerated people the opportunity to be accountable and make plans for how they might work toward repairing the harm they have caused their loved ones and others.

Even if someone did not commit a crime and is wrongly imprisoned, which is the case for some people in the United States,[15] an innocent person can address how s/he might reconcile with that injustice. One woman who maintains her innocence wanted a Circle to address how she could reconcile with loved ones who abandoned her years before, early after her conviction.[16] *The Innocence Project*, which represents her, a prison representative, and her sister (whom she had not seen in 20 years since going to prison at age 18) attended her Circle. The woman's plan for reconciliation, as could be for any unjustly imprisoned person, includes legal remedies along with other ways to cope with imprisonment. Additionally the families of innocent people wrongly incarcerated have been affected, and they too can benefit from this process. The children of the wrongly convicted and incarcerated woman said, it was "helpful" that they were contacted and interviewed by telephone and allowed to participate in the Circle this way.

---

[15] Over 90% of all convicted felons in the United States pled guilty, therefore, we can assume many imprisoned people committed some offense.

[16] In addition to the innocent woman in Hawai'i, a Nigerian woman was wrongly imprisoned in Finland and benefitted from a Circle held there for her and her immediate family.

We cannot change the past. No one can alter past negative behavior, and no one can control other people's behavior, but people can influence their own futures, and choose how they will respond to both their own negative behavior and others'. Most people who want Circles are troubled with guilt and shame that they have hurt their loved ones and other people. The Circles allow them to address these feelings that can become self-destructive left unaddressed. Even if a loved one does not attend, as in the Modified Circles, making a plan for how to repair the harm can alleviate some guilt and shame. Making amends even when a harmed person does not know about it, can help the wrongdoer focus on the future and what they can do to live a crime and drug free life, instead of focusing on guilt.

Psychologist Albert Eglash is thought to have "coined the phrase restorative justice" (Bazemore). In his 1977 paper he discusses rehabilitation benefits for people who have committed crimes including the value of "making amends" with people harmed (Eglash, 1977, p. 93).

Shame is one of the most difficult human emotions. We all do things at times that hurt others, either intentionally or accidentally. At times we are all guilty of bad behavior and we justify our bad acts. People with high levels of self-esteem justify themselves more frequently than others with less (Tavris & Aronson, 2007). Our justifications allow us to avoid the *cognitive dissonance* we feel when we err, and keep us from addressing our shame. Psychologists Carol Tavris and Elliot Aronson wrote *Mistakes Were Made (but not by me): Why We Justify Foolish Beliefs, Bad Decisions, and Hurtful Acts* to explain cognitive dissonance, and how it naturally motivates self-justification, often creating further problems especially when used to justify continuing harmful behaviors.

> Cognitive dissonance is a state of tension that occurs whenever a person holds two cognitions (ideas, attitudes, beliefs, opinions) that are psychologically inconsistent, such as 'Smoking is a dumb thing to do because it could kill me' and 'I smoke two packs a day.' Dissonance produces mental discomfort, ranging from minor pangs to deep anguish; people don't rest easy until they find a way to reduce it." (Tavris & Aronson, 2007, p. 13).

A smoker can reduce her cognitive dissonance by quitting, or using self-justification. "My Aunt Minnie smoked everyday and lived to be 95," or "I gain too much weight when I don't smoke." Justifying our behaviors protects us from seeing that what we are doing is harmful. In cases of violence, justification can lead to further violence. "Aggression begets self-justification, which begets

43

more aggression." Tavris and Aronson discuss people who have taken responsibility for serious mistakes: "These courageous individuals take us straight into the heart of dissonance and its innermost irony: The mind wants to protect itself from the pain of dissonance with the balm of self-justification; but the soul wants to confess" (Tavris & Aronson p. 27).

The Circles provide incarcerated people with the opportunity "to confess" and express their shame. Circles help reintegrate people back into their families and community. Reintegrative shame is more effective for changing behavior than stigmatizing shame, which occurs when a person is distinguished for her bad nature, e.g. the wrongdoer holds a sign that says: "I am a welfare cheat." This public display puts the wrongdoer outside the group. In contrast, the Circle's focus is on the effects of bad behavior and imprisonment, *never a person\s bad essence or nature.* This aspect of the process allows the incarcerated person to continue or regain status as an accepted member of the community after the group discusses what could be done to repair the harm. Continued membership in the group makes it more likely that the offender will conform to the community's standards in the future. This *communitarianism* element of the conference is necessary for preventing repeat offenses (Braithwaite, 1989).

Incarcerated people can address how they might repair harm their behavior caused for people not present at the Circle. Reconciliation does not require contact between the people who committed the crime and the people directly or indirectly hurt by it. Reconciliation does not require a restoration of relationships. Often there is no relationship to restore. Often crime victims are unknown and unrelated to offenders. Irrespective of repaired relationships, incarcerated people can plan how to make things right with the non-participating community at large, and Circle participants.

B. Reconciliation Stage of Circle

The facilitator introduces the reconciliation stage of the Circle by telling the group that the incarcerated person's desire for the Circle shows that she takes responsibility for herself, which is another one of her strengths. The reconciliation stage of the Circle is highly emotional and many tears are usually shed.

The reconciliation portion of the Circle ask three basic restorative justice questions: 1. Who was affected by the past misbehavior and incarceration? 2. How were they affected? and 3. What might be done to repair the harm? The incarcerated person answers the first two questions, "Who was affected, and how?" After the incarcerated person speaks, the facilitator asks, "Back then when you did those things," (invariably the discussion touches on what the incarcerated person did), "what were you thinking?" After the person explains with something like, "I was selfish and just thinking about myself," the facilitator asks, "and what do you think now about what you did, and what you were thinking back then?"

Asking the person to reflect on their past behavior, is an important rehabilitation opportunity. It is a chance for the incarcerated person to share their insight and to describe how they have changed, and "transformed" their life from "crime" to law abiding (Maruna, 2001). Sharing their transformation with others, and hearing themselves say it, can strengthen and reaffirm their commitment to better future behavior (Jenkins, 1990).

Next the focus shifts to the loved ones. Those present, or from printed statements of telephonic interviews of loved ones not present, share how they were affected by the prior behavior and incarceration, and what could be done to repair the harm. One universal condition that almost all loved ones want is for the incarcerated person to stay away from drugs and alcohol if that was an issue in the past. When an incarcerated person says that s/he will not drink again or use drugs anymore, s/he is asked by the facilitator: "What gives you hope you can stay clean and sober? You probably tried to quit using in the past. What is different about this time?" The SF scaling technique is particularly useful here where the facilitator asks "On a scale of 1 to 10, where are you on staying clean and sober?" Regardless of where the incarcerated individual says they are on the scale, it is an important opportunity to recognize positive steps they have already made towards sobriety, and find ways they can continue. It is also a good opportunity to discuss it with loved ones who often are skeptical of their newly found commitment. The facilitator can address this skepticism by asking: "What do you know about yourself now that [name of loved one present] does not know about you?"

Not surprisingly, many incarcerated people agree to either stop drugs or alcohol use altogether or reduce its harmful effects. Only one person in the 66 Circles to date has refused to say s/he would never drink again. This individual was a young man (YM) in his twenties. His sisters wanted him to give up drinking completely and he refused. After a discussion about why they wanted him to quit drinking, and his drug treatment counselor's strong recommendation that he follow his sisters' wishes, he said:

> YM: "I'm sorry I can't sit here say I will never drink again, because I am probably going to. I am not sure I will, but I can't say I won't. I can't lie to you."

F: "Not lying is really important to you, and you want to be honest with your sisters."

YM: [looking at his sisters] "Yeah, I want to tell you the truth and I cannot honestly say I won't drink again."

Using SFBT techniques the facilitator helped reframe his refusal into a strength, and his honesty lent him some credibility with his family.

Being honest was something that the young man and his sisters agreed was necessary to restore their relationships and help repair the harm. His sisters knew he was being honest notwithstanding his refusal to never drink again, and it grounded him into seeing himself as an honest person. Five years after his Circle the young man was back in prison, and estranged from his sisters. One sister reported that regardless of "his choices, the Circle process was definitely healing" for her family and they remain satisfied that they participated in it despite their brother's re-incarceration. "He's always been really hardheaded. Maybe he'll get it someday," his sister said hopefully.

C. Reconciliation with Unrelated People & the Community At Large

Most people who have Circles see that their prior behavior has not only hurt their loved ones, but recognize that it has also hurt unrelated people whose identity they may never know, e.g., theft victims, community members who suffered from drug dealing in their neighborhoods, taxpayers who paid the cost of incarceration, etc. At their Circles they agree to do things like "Pay back the community, by doing service and volunteer" work when they are released. But the most common way people having Circles say they will make amends to their unknown victims is by "walking the talk." They plan to remain substance free and law abiding in the future to reconcile with the community and with their loved ones. A few incarcerated people who had Circles, have listed "obeying prison rules" as one way to walk the talk, and make amends to the community while being incarcerated.

Additionally, repairing harm caused to deceased people has also been addressed at Circles. Law abiding and clean and sober living, have been dedicated to late grandparents, parents, and others by some incarcerated people. As with meeting other needs addressed in the Circle, reconciliation also includes determining concrete actions and a timeline for when the actions will be completed, .e.g. "Kathy will write an apology letter to Grandmother by January 12, 2011."

D. Apologies & Forgiveness

Most people who have Circles openly apologize to their loved ones attending. Often it is agreed that the incarcerated person will prepare a written apology to others not at the Circle. During their interview for the Circle, facilitators may say, "Forgiveness is a gift and you don't ask for gifts." An apology on the other hand is something that an incarcerated person can give to another person.

When incarcerated people agree to make apologies, a free apology letter writing program available on the Internet, www.apologyletter.org, is suggested as a tool (Furman & Walker, 2010). This simple and confidential computer program assists people in making a meaningful, restorative and solution-focused apologies.[17] Because nternet use is prohibited by the Hawai'i prison system, the apology letter guidelines are printed out for incarcerated people to use for preparing apologies as planned at their Circles when requested. See Appendix G for the Restorative Apology Letter Guidelines.

One person who used the apology letter guidelines, had violently killed someone 20 years earlier. The closest relative of the deceased, who was unrelated to the incarcerated person, was not at the Circle. The imprisoned person, along with their Circle supporters, believed an apology letter might be helpful to the deceased's relative. Before the apology letter was sent, the facilitator contacted the victim's relative and asked for permission to send it. With the relative's agreement, the letter was sent, along with a letter from the facilitator, explaining the Circle program and saying she believed the person was appeared genuinely sorry for their terrible violence. The letter also offered a facilitated meeting between the relative and the incarcerated person if the relative ever wished. Expanding the Circle program to include providing victim/offender dialogues and other restorative practices to deal with outstanding problems is an eventual hope.

When apologies are made to people who are unrelated, and it is determined the prior crimes are not so serious as to warrant seeking permission to send them, e.g. non-violent minor theft, and the victims are related, a prison staff representative, such as the incarcerated person's drug treatment counselor or spiritual advisor, can sign a statement that they reviewed the apology letter and that they believe it was written sincerely.

---

[17] The www.apologyletter.org program also provides programs for people to deal with hardship, and to explore and imagine forgiveness for others and themselves.

Loved ones also apologize during the Circles. In one Circle the mother of the incarcerated man said: "I owe you an apology son. I'm so sorry I first got you into drugs. It was me that gave you it. It was wrong of me. I am so ashamed. I'm in my recovery now. I want to do all I can to support you in yours." Many family and friends also extend forgiveness to their loved ones who invited them to the Circles. Some incarcerated people identify, "Self-forgiveness is something I need."[18]

The conclusion of the reconciliation segment ends with the incarcerated person answering, "Is there anything you want to say right now before we close the reconciliation part of the Circle?" Everyone whose had a Circle has said something remorseful and/or thankful at the conclusion of the reconciliation stage of their Circles.

5. Circle Break after Reconciliation Stage of Circle

By the time the reconciliation stage is complete it has been about two hours since the Circle began. There has been a lot of emotional discussion, and people are tired. This is an ideal time for a short 5 - 10 minute break before the next steps in the Circle.

6. Specifying What the Incarcerated Person Wants Different in Their Future

After the reconciliation stage and break, the incarcerated person is asked: "How do you want your future to be different from your past?" This is to identify goals, but because some people get anxious about not having goals, the question is asked indirectly.

Most imprisoned people have had drug and alcohol problems. Most say they want, "A clean and sober life" in the future. This presents another opportunity to use solution-focused questions: "What gives you hope you can achieve this?" A scaling question may be asked, "On a scale of 0 to 10, 0 you relapse and 10 you stay clean, where are you honestly?" After a number is identified they are asked, "Why aren't you at a lower point?" And "What would it take for you to move up a point?" If they say 10, the question is, "What can you do to be 110% sure you can stay clean?"

When people say, "Don't use drugs" is a goal, it is reframed into a positive statement like, "Stay clean and sober." Vague ideas like, "Stay on the right path," are made concrete. "What would we see you doing when you are on the right path?" All efforts are made to make goals concrete and

---

[18] Forgiveness is taught as a life skill as explained by Fred Luskin, Ph.D. in *Forgive for Good* which has been provided for many incarcerated people in Hawai'i through the Circle and 12 week solution-focused restorative practices programs.

precise. We want everyone to be clear about what exactly that the incarcerated person wants for himself or herself in their future, and what work s/he needs to do to achieve those goals.

7. Making Plans for Meeting Practical Needs

After identifying the incarcerated person's goals, other practical needs are addressed including: housing, employment, transportation, necessary documents (i.e. social security card, birth certificate, etc.), maintaining emotional and physical health, listing their supporters, and deciding on a date for a follow up Circle. Also any unique needs of the incarcerated person are addressed e.g., paying child support, obtaining a divorce, locating a missing child, etc.

A. Housing

Having a place to live is absolutely vital for everyone leaving prison. The Circles always ask the group to help generate at least three alternative housing choices. Some incarcerated people whose families offer their homes for them to live after release, prefer to live other places, and do not want to be dependent on their parents. They typically say something like, "I need to do this myself. I want to do it on my own and show I can do it without help. I always lean on them and this time I'm not." Even if a housing option is "certain," such as "going to live back at home with parents," two more alternatives are determined. The Transition Plan will also indicate if any housing plans are subject to parole board approval.

Planning for Housing Needs

F: "Three alternative housing options need to be included in Kathy's plan. Even if you have one place set up, we need two back up places. Since you're going to the parole board, it's up to them to decide where you will live regardless of what you want. So what are you planning for where you will live Kathy?

K: "With my daughters in Kaneohe's."

F: [looking at Kathy's daughters (KD)] "Is that right, your mom can come and live with you in Kaneohe's?"

KD: "Yes, absolutely, we have room for her. It's her old house. We all talked about it and are planning for her to come home. Her stuff is all still where she left it."

F: "Okay so if it doesn't work with your daughters for any reason, where is your second choice to live after your release Kathy?

K: "I don't know. I could get my own apartment."

F: "Is that realistic? Do you have the money to rent your own place?"

K: "Not yet, I don't. After I work though and save money."

F: "Great, you can do that after you save money. Does anyone else have ideas where else she could live?"

L: [Kathy's friend Liz attending Circle] "How bout a clean and sober house?"

F: [looking at Kathy] "Is that something you'd like? Live in a clean and sober house?"

K: "Yeah, I could do that."

F: "Okay, great. Now which one?"

K: "I don't know."

F: "How can you find a clean and sober house?"

E: [Earl who works for the prison and is Kathy's case manager] "She can go see Carlo in the prison law library and get the list of houses from him. The she needs to write the houses about vacancies and see if one will take her by the date she is released."

F: Great Earl. Can you do that [looking at Kathy]? Go get the list from Carlo and write the houses about vacancies?"

K: "Yes."

F: Okay by what date can you go see Carlo and get the list of houses from him?"

K: "I can put in my request tonight and go next Wednesday."

F: "Great. How many letters do you think you need to write?"

E: "She should write at least 10 I think."

F: "Okay, can you write 10 letters?"

K: "I can write one and make copies in the law library."

F: By what date can you do that and then mail them by?"

K: "By Friday, I think."

F: "What date can you do it for sure Kathy? And do you needs stamps, paper, envelopes or anything else to write and mail the letters?"

K: For sure by next Monday then, and yeah, I have stamps and everything to do the letters."

As much detail as necessary to describe exactly what, and by when, the incarcerated person will do is gathered by the facilitator. It is vital that the Transition Plan be as concrete as possible to establish what the expectations are, helping to ensure success in carrying out the plan. This is important for the family and the incarcerated person. The more success the incarcerated person experiences in achieving the Plan's goals and outcomes, the more confidence will develop in the incarcerated person.

Often incarcerated people go to live with their family. In these cases a facilitator can offer the group the opportunity to develop a behavioral contract so everyone knows what the expectations are if the incarcerated person lives in the family home. A behavioral contract can help make the living arrangement successful and avoid conflicts. The following is a sample conversation which would take place during this phase of the Circle if participants indicate it would be helpful. See Appendix I for an example behavioral contract.

Discussing Creating a Behavioral Contract

F: "Okay your daughter is welcome to come live with you in your home. What are your hopes for her living there? What are your expectations for her behavior with her living there?"

Parent (P): "Just that she stay with the program, be a mother to her kids and stay on the right path."

F: "What do you mean exactly when you expect her to *stay with the program*?"

P: "That she keep doing what she's doing."

F: "Which is what? What is she doing that you want her to keep doing, to live in your home?"

P: "I want her staying off drugs and away from the bad influences she hooks up with that bring her down."

F: "And staying off of drugs, what behavior do you want her to have that is staying off drugs?"

P: "I want her to stay clean and sober."

F: "Okay, you want her to stay clean and sober. What do you mean stay away from the bad influences?"

P: "Those people at the beach she leaves with that use and bring her down every time."

F: "Who are those people exactly?"

P: "That guy called Hairball, I know one is called, he's always hanging out at 7-Eleven, and Melissa, she's known since intermediate school. They all live down there on the beach."

F: [looking at incarcerated person (IP)] "Are those things you can do? Stay clean and sober, and away from Hairball and Melissa and the other people your mom is talking about?"

IP: "Yeah for sure. I'm not going back to that. I'm keeping my 50 feet distance from them. It'll be "Hi and Bye" when I see em'. That's it."

F: [looking at parent] Are there other things you want your daughter to do to live at your home? Like pay rent, do certain chores?"

P: "No, no rent. She's just gonna be getting on her feet. She always does chores. Everyone in the house does. With all of us living there, and then her, we need to all pitch in and make sure things get done."

F: "Great everyone pitches in and helps out, very cooperative family. What chores exactly would she be expected to do?"

P: "I need her to help with the kids after school, take em to their activities. Kimo has football practice, and Anna is in soccer."

F: [looking at IP] "Is that something you can do, take the kids to these activities""

IP: "I would love to take care of my kids. I will do whatever is needed for them."

F: [look at IP's mother] "What other chores would you like her to do to stay in your home? And we can put this all in a behavioral agreement that we can attach to the written Circle Summary and Transition Plan we will be mailing to you recording what was decided today. The agreement can help everyone remember what Kathy needs to do to help out the family if she is living there."

Families report years later how helpful it was to have a behavioral contract, "We had it stuck on the refrigerator. Every Tuesday and Thursday he did the yard work. We never had to ask him," reported one mother. A poignant example of their power was of one man returned home to stay in his old bedroom. While formulated the behavioral contact he asked his mother at a Circle, "Please check up inside that green lamp shade mom. I stashed some dope in there and don't want it there when I come home."

B. Financial and Employment

Many incarcerated people are economically disadvantaged and struggle to make ends meet when they are back in the community. Money and employment needs must be met for most to successfully transition. Sometimes there will be a savings, but most often people will rely on family or welfare for a few months after being released while they look for jobs. In discussing employment and financial assistance, specifics and details are vital. The more specific the information discussed and included in the plan, the less likely there will be misunderstandings or a need will not be met after release.

Discussing Financial and Employment Needs

F: "What kind of work do you do Kathy?"

K: "I work in hotels, at Ko'Olina, in the household department. My boss said I can have my job back. She wrote me a letter."

F: "Great you already have a job lined up! Just in case something happens and your Ko'Olina job doesn't work out, where else could you work?"

K: "I dunno. Gonna have to find a job."

F: "What exactly do you need to do to find a job? And does anyone else have ideas for Kathy, about what can she do to find a job?

L: "She can go to Worknet and apply. They're a awesome help. She can do her resume with them and even get clothes from them after she gets out for interviews."

F: "Great, how can she get in touch with Worknet?"

K: "Oh hey yeah, I'm in it! It's part of Lifestyles, I'm level III now. I even got some tokens to use."

F: "Good for you Kathy! What are the tokens for?"

K: "For stuff like buying clothes, tuition and I forget what else."

F: "Okay, when can you find out what Lifestyles can help you with exactly Kathy?'

K: "My Lifestyles class is on Thursday. I can ask Chaz about stuff then."

F: "Okay great. You are going to ask him about how many tokens you have earned, what they can get you and what else the program can do for you after you get out."

K: "Yeah I know I think I can be in level IV when I get out."

F: "Okay great Kathy, you can ask Chaz about level four too by Thursday, we'll put that in your plan okay?" [Kathy nods her head up and down]

After making plans for employment, the facilitator guides the group back to ways Kathy can get some financial assistance immediately after her release.

L: "You can go to the library too and use the computer terminals there for free."....

F: "If Kathy returns right to work even a few days after her release it will be a few or more before she gets a pay check, what can she do in the meantime for money?"

L: "I am glad to help her out with some help. I don't have a lot but I can give her enough to get some of her necessaries."

F: "Are there any other ways Kathy might be able to get some financial assistance the first few weeks of her release?"

E: "She can apply for public assistance. Welfare is available for anyone coming out who doesn't have a savings. She just has to go fill out an application on line anytime after her release."

F: "Thanks Earl. Kathy is that something you're interested in? Applying for public assistance?"

K: "Yeah sure. I guess I can use Liz's computer, yeah Liz?

L: "Of course you can use mine anytime Kath."

C. Transportation

Transportation is essential. Incarcerated people must be able to get to meetings for parole officers, job interviews, and meet their other obligations. Kathy like most, decided the bus would be her main method of transportation, and her friend Liz also volunteered to give her rides when possible. It is useful to brain storm possible car share resources and public transportation options.

D. Documents

Incarcerated people in Hawai'i and most other state prisons are not allowed to have their personal documents in their possession while imprisoned. An original social security card is usually necessary to work at most places. If it is lost a new one must be ordered from the federal social security office. A picture identification and birth certificate are necessary to obtain a duplicate social security card. Sometimes all documents are lost when one is imprisoned and all need to be ordered. Sometimes parents or other loved ones volunteer to order them before their release and have them sent to their homes to speed up the process. Other times, the process simply must wait until after release. Whatever the situation it must be discussed and a plan for obtaining the documents needs to be made before release.

E. Life Long Learning & Education

The need for continued learning is an important need for everyone. Some Circle observers have commented that it was helpful for them also to recognize their needs for continued learning. Meeting the need for life long learning can lead to meaningful work and positive use of leisure time. Life long learning does not have to be college or higher education. It can be anything that a person is interested in learning about. The goal is to get the incarcerated person to identify what they are interested in learning about to keep them engaged in a meaningful life. People who have had Circles have discussed a wide range of interests from motorcycle maintenance to medical care.

Discussing Life Long Learning & Education

F: Another need you have like all humans have is the need for continued learning Kathy. What are you interested in that you want to learn more about?"

K: "I want to become a CSAC and help youth."

F: "Okay and that's a *certified substance abuse counselor*, a CSCA right?" [Kathy nods her head yes, up and down] "Okay, what do you need to do to become a CSCA?" [Kathy looks puzzled and shakes her head no, from side to side].

L: "She needs to take the classes and put in the time. I am working on it right now.".......

F: "Great Liz. Where would Kathy go take the classes and get more information about the requirements?"

L: "From the department of health. They test everyone and give out all the requirements. The address is in the phone book."

F: "Great Kathy can you look at a phone book somewhere here and write DOH for the CSAC requirements?"

K: "Yeah the law library has one."

F: "When can you get the address and write the letter and mail it by?"

K: "I could do it by next Friday."

F: "Is there anything else you are interested in learning more about?"

K: "I would like to learn more about how to be a better mother."

F: "How can you do that?"

K: "I could take more parenting classes here."

F: "Great, when can you enroll in one?"

K: "I have to ask about that, I'm not sure."

E: "I think we're going to have some new courses on parenting next month. I can check and let you know."

F: "Thanks Earl. By what date can you let Kathy know about the parenting course?"

E: "I can let her know by next Wednesday."

F. Maintaining Physical Health

How one will maintain health is essential to successful reentry. Usually a healthy diet and exercise are the two main areas addressed here. Sometimes incarcerated individuals have already begun to take steps to maintain physical health while inside prison. Some prisons have fitness programming which incarcerated individuals can take advantage of. If someone has a special medical need too, for example, asthma or diabetes, etc., those needs are also addressed.

Discussing Maintaining Physical Health

F: "Kathy what do you need to do to maintain good physical health?"

K: "Eat right."

F: "What exactly does eat right mean?"

K: "Eat the right kind of food for healthiness."

F: "What kind of foods are the right kind for you to eat for healthiness?"

K: "Fish and chicken, no junk food, or candies and sweets and no carbs."

L: "And you gotta eat veggies and fruits too Kath!"

F: "What else do you need to do to maintain good health Kathy or does anyone else have ideas?"

L: "She needs to work out."

K: "Oh, yeah, I gotta keep working out for myself."

F: "What exactly do you need to do to work out Kathy?"

K: "Power walk, do some sit ups and stuff."

F: "Okay great. What will be realistic for you to do weekly after your release do you think? What is the minimum about of time and how many times a weeks can you do it?

K: "Power walk everyday for an hour."

F: "Will that be realistic if you are working?"

K: "Yes, I have to do an hour everyday. Well maybe not on Sundays."

F: "Okay then Monday through Saturday, and a whole hour? Or is there another number that is something you can do for sure?

K: "I guess at least 30 minutes and if I have more time I can do the hour."

F: "Okay and for the sit-ups. How many will you do and how many days a week?"

K: "I do 250 every other day."

F: "Will that be realistic after you're released? If not, what's a minimum number?"

K: "At least 100 3x a week."

G. Maintaining Emotional Health

This aspect of reentry is especially important for people who have the goal to remain clean and sober. Substance abuse is often motivated by undesirable emotions and addressing how to maintain emotional health can help prevent relapse. Ways of maintaining emotional health mentioned in the Circles include, reading daily, writing in journals, getting a sponsor (e.g. AA or NA sponsor), listening to music, and doing exercise. Sometimes people mention counseling and therapy too. Identifying therapists is always necessary when this is mentioned, or finding a way to find a good therapist if a specific one has not been identified should be explored.

Planning who is in a support group upon release is another way an incarcerated person can maintain emotional health is addressed specifically in the process. Having the Circle early on in the imprisonment period helps to solidify supporters. Most of the people at the Circle readily volunteer to be in the support group. Making the commitment during the Circle with witnesses to provide support, makes it more likely the individuals will follow through. Answering, "Who can you call when you need help?" is how an incarcerated person identifies her/his support group.

Discussing Maintaining Emotional Health

F: "Kathy what do you need to do to keep your emotional health good?"

K: "My devotionals are something I have to do everyday to keep my head screwed on right."

F: "What exactly do you do when you do your devotionals and how often do you do them?"

K: "I pray, and read the Bible, and self-help books every morning. Takes me about 30 minutes and that's how I start my day in a good mood."

F: "Wow great Kathy! You practice doing what you need to maintain a good mood, you have good insight into yourself. What else do you need to do for good emotional health?"

K: "Stay connected to my family and don't isolate myself. I gotta stay clean, that's most important."

F: "Good to stay connected to your family. How often do you need to connect with your family?"

K: "Everyday I need to talk to them all."

L: "What about NA too Kath? I think you need to go to meetings."

K: "Yeah I need to go to meetings too."

F: "How often do you think you need to go to meetings Kathy? And are they AA or NA meetings or either?"

K: "I like NA. Everyday I think I need to go."

L: "Yeah, 30 meetings in 30 days after your release for sure Kath. That's the formula."

K: "Okay I can do that, maybe even 60 meetings in 60 days!"

F: "What is realistic?"

H. Addressing Other Unique Needs

Each incarcerated person has unique needs and sometimes these needs are specifically discussed. Examples include filing for a divorce, locating children whose custody was lost due to the imprisonment (sadly this is automatic in many instances after 18 months of imprisonment). These unique needs should be addressed and included in the Transition Plan with timelines established for taking any necessary actions.

Discussing Other Unique Needs

F: "You said that you wanted to file for a divorce from your husband Kathy. Is that something we need to discuss and that you need to make a plan for doing?"

K: "Okay, yeah I want to get it legalized, the divorce. We haven't been together for about 3 years and won't be again, but I should get it all done official with the courts and law."

F: "Does anyone have ideas about how she can get a divorce or start the proceedings while she is incarcerated?"

L: "I just did my own with the court's help. They have a desk at the second floor of Family Court and the people helped me fill out all the forms, Kathy could do that."

F: "Great, how can you get the court's help while you're here in prison Kathy?"

K: "I guess I could write and ask them."

F: "Sounds like a good idea. I can get you the address for the Family Court. By what date do you want to write and mail that letter?"

K: "How about by the end of the month?"

---

8. Setting the Re-Circle Date

Plans change and people will have feedback about how their plans are carried out and what else they need to do for a successful reentry after their first Circle. The follow up *Re-Circle* is an important date to set. The group simply decides when the best time would be to schedule the followup Re-Circle. Sometimes it is six months later or after the person is released from prison.

Normally it is left to the incarcerated person to contact the facilitator to schedule the followup Circle, but ideally programs should provide resources for facilitators or recorders to contact the incarcerated person is s/he fails to contact them about the re-Circle. Continued interest in their life and plans, and how things are going, can only be helpful for promoting desistance from crime and staying clean and sober.

Followup with Re-Circles has been the major shortcoming of the Hawai'i program because it is basically run on small grants and *pro bono* efforts. There have been few re-Circles due to a lack of resources. Out of the 66 full Circles provided to date only four have had follow up re-Circles.

9. Closing Circle

After each of the needs have been addressed, the Circle closes by asking each person starting with the prison staff person first to:"Please compliment Kathy on anything you learned about her today or on any changes you've noticed about her."

Any compliments that identify new strengths not mentioned previously are included in the written Circle Summary and listed under the strengths section. For example, someone may say the incarcerated person was "brave" for having a Circle and that will be included in the list of her strengths.

Lastly, Kathy is asked to: "Please close today's Circle by saying how this process was for you or anything else you want to say." This is usually a very moving part of the Circle. There is a lot of heart-felt emotion and gratitude shared by the incarcerated person for the people coming to her Circle. Tissue are always needed at most Circles because there is a lot of crying.

10. Surveys and Data Collection

After the Circle ends individuals are asked to fill out a one-page survey documenting their Circle experience. Please see Appendix J for a sample of participant surveys. Programs need feedback to maintain effectiveness and these are usually pilot projects. Surveys and evaluations are important to learn from to improve the process, and to justify resources and future funding. All programs should strive to become more effective. The learning curve for improving group processes and Circles should never end for the people administering and providing the programs.

11. Breaking of Bread

Sharing food at the end of a restorative process between the participants is an important feature and an ancient human symbol for healing. Humans do not eat together if there is a lot of animosity and other negative emotions. If the prison allows it, refreshments of cookies and juice, tea and coffee are provided while surveys are being filled out. There is also usually a short time for the participants to informally socialize after the Circle. Normally the Circles are scheduled for three hours, and whatever time is remaining after the surveys is left for the participants to socialize. This period for informal socialization is also important for debriefing for any observers, which often there are.

Step 6: Circle Summary and Transition Plan Preparation and Delivery to Participants

The recorder is copying as much as possible during the Circle and the facilitator is also filling in a blank Circle Summary and Transition Plan. See Appendix F for a Circle Summary and Transition Plan blank sample and Appendix G for a filled in sample. Within at least five working days after a Circle, the Summary is typed out on a computer and copies are sent to the incarcerated person, each household that participated in the Circle, and the prison staff representative. Normally, the Summary and Plan are about six pages in length. When the Summary and Plan are delivered to the prison staff person, usually by fax or emailed as a PDF file, it is asked that the Summary also be provided to the parole board representative who collects important documents at each Hawai'i state prison. Each jurisdiction can address which agencies need to receive a copy of the Summary and Plan.

Many incarcerated people over the years who have had either a full or Modified Circle have commented on how helpful it is to have this written plan. "Seeing I did what I said I would do, really gave me confidence!" is a typical response to the value of having the written Summary and Plan.

Part Three: Creating A Reentry and Transition Planning Circle Process in Your Community

I. Developing Facilitators & Recorders

A. Training

1. Facilitators

The first step in developing this process in your community is having interested parties trained in the process. Comprehensive training is critical to understanding the nuances of this unique process. Ideally, facilitators attend a 24-hour training provided over three or four days. The training is conducted in circles and includes applied learning activities. A Circle may be observed, if possible to arrange with a prison, on the first afternoon of the training. If going to the prison and watching an actual Circle is not possible, finding someone recently released from prison, parole, probation, or a substance abuse treatment facility to come to the training to have either a Modified Circle without their loved ones, or a full Circle including loved ones, is a good alternative. Having prospective facilitators observe an actual Circle at the beginning of the training gives them a solid understanding of what the process is all about.

After the 24-hour training, the facilitator trainees observe at least two interviews in the prison. After watching the interviews, where trainees are also invited to asked solution-focused questions, the trainees observe the convening of a Circle.

To learn how to convene the Circles, the trainee listens to the telephone conversations while a supervising facilitator contacts the people the incarcerated person listed as potential participants. Next the trainee observes at least two Circles in the prison. While observing the Circles, the trainee fills out an observation form, which helps her engage in the process. The survey that an observer completes is attached as Appendix K. The form also gives the trainee something to relate to afterwards, when she de-briefs with the facilitator and recorder. The debriefing takes about one hour to go over the important occurrences of the Circles. Two people can be trained together and share in discussions and debriefing with the supervising facilitator.

After observing two Circles, the facilitator trainee is ready to record Circles. After recording at least two Circles, or as long as the lead facilitator believes is necessary for the trainee to understand the process sufficiently, the trainee is ready to interview applicants under the supervision of the lead facilitator. The lead facilitator will supervise the trainee facilitator for at least two Circles and record with the trainee for two more Circles before the trainee is left to facilitate without supervision. Every person is unique and training time will depend on each individual.

2. Recorders

Circle recorders preform an important role in the Circle by collecting the participants' information that will become part of the written Circle Summary and Transition Plan. Many recorders go on to become Circle facilitators after a few months, but some prefer to remain in the role of the recorder. The recorders take the same 24 hour training the facilitators do and are supervised by the facilitator during the Circles.

Recorders provide feedback to facilitators and help provide the Circle. In Hawai'i the recorders bring the large sheets of paper to attach to the walls for recording, felt pens for writing, and copies of participant surveys and pens to fill them out after the Circle. If the prison where the Circles are held allows refreshments, the recorder is also responsible for providing them. The recorder debriefs with the facilitator after each Circle on the process, and if any unexpected incidents that occur during the Circle, she informs the program coordinator about them.

3. Listening Skill Training

Listening skills are key for facilitators and recorders providing this reentry and transition planning process. Role playing Circles are a large part of the facilitator training along with at least four hours of listening skill development including learning how to apply the *Compassionate Listening* model (Hwoschinsky, 2001), and *mindful listening*. Compassionate Listening recognizes that what people feel is important for healing, and that identifying what people value is important for recognizing their strengths and dealing with hostility.

Mindful listening as described and taught to others by Lorenn Walker is based on the Buddhist practice of *mindful meditation*. Mindfulness has been applied to psychology as a therapeutic intervention to assist troubled people, and *cognitive restructuring*, popular in many prison rehabilitation programs today, is recognized to have roots in Buddhist practice. (Ellis, 1999).

Jon Kabat-Zinn received a Ph.D. in molecular biology from the Massachusetts Institute of Technology. As a professor of medicine at the University of Massachusetts he founded the world-renown *Stress Reduction Clinic*. He is also the author of numerous books on learning mindfulness meditation, and applying mindfulness to daily living. Kabat-Zinn says:

> Mindfulness means paying attention in a particular way: on purpose, in the present moment, and nonjudgmentally. This kind of attention nurtures greater awareness, clarity, and acceptance of present-moment reality. It wakes us up to the fact that our lives unfold only in moments. If we are not fully present for many of those moments, we may not only miss what is most valuable in our lives but also fail to realize the richness and depth of our possibilities for growth and transformation" (Kabat-Zinn, 1994, p.4).

Mindful Listening applies these concepts and is learned and increased by practicing being fully engaged in whoever is speaking and not in one's own thoughts. Mindful Listening is about giving another person your whole attention.

Mindful listening is embodied in the words of Henri Nouwen:

> True listeners no longer have an inner need to make their presence known. They are free to receive, to welcome, to accept. Listening is much more than allowing another to talk while waiting for a chance to respond. Listening is paying full attention to others and welcoming them into our very beings. The beauty of listening is that those who are listened to start feeling accepted, start taking their words more seriously and discovering their true selves. Listening is a form of spiritual hospitality by which you invite strangers to become friends, to get to know their inner selves more fully, and even to dare to be silent with you (Nouwen, p. 74).

Compassionate Listening, also rigorously taught to Circle facilitators and recorders, is also derived from Buddhism, and specifically from the teachings of the Vietnamese monk Thich Nhat Hanh (Green, 2010). Compassionate Listening is an exercise in identifying someone's values (positive motivations) feelings, and specific facts of their situation. When someone is complaining, angry or even hostile, beneath their troubled state there is something positive that they value. Imagine the angry and hostile feelings of a mother whose daughter has relapsed and is back in prison for the third time. The daughter has again left her three young children in the care of their grandmother. The positive value beneath the grandmother's anger could be that she values parenting and wants the best for her grandchildren. The mother believes that her imprisoned daughter has the capability to be a good parent. Her hostility is based on these positive values. Recognizing an upset person's positive values and motivations underlying their anger and frustration, helps to defuse their misery and can provide them some healing. When Circle facilitators help identify these values there is increased understanding and peace between people, and within individuals too.

Listening skills are also key for facilitators in learning and applying solution-building language. One of the most important tenants of solution-focused brief therapy is that every individual is the expert of their own lives. Individuals, no matter what sort of problems they face, know more about their capacities and goals than anyone else, including highly educated and experienced professionals and experts working with them. To become skilled at applying solution-building language takes a lot of practice in concentrated listening. Efforts to improve listening skills have lasting value not only for those who are listened to in this way, but for the practitioner also.

4. Solution Focused Brief Therapy Training

The use of solution focused brief therapy (SFBT), as described here is a critical aspect of this group process. Therapists who utilize SFBT undergo extensive training in its practices and theory. Since Circle facilitators are not acting in the role of therapists, the SFBT training necessary to facilitate a Circle is abbreviated and targeted to specific tools, which are useful for Circle facilitation (see "SFBT technique highlight" sections page of this workbook).

Solution-focused practices require the facilitator to move away from a problem solving paradigm, which examines the problem in depth and mainly analyzes maladaptive behavior. This can be a particularly difficult task for facilitators who have a background in social work, law, and traditional therapy. Often, these professions place emphasis on the past behavior and problem rather than the coping skills and strengths of individuals. In this way, the SFBT approach "is simple to learn, but difficult to practice because our old learning gets in the way" (Berg, undated). American culture generally teaches us to focus on problems and what we do not want, rather than identifying what we do want and finding ways to achieve goals.

Programs administering this Circle process should strive to provide ongoing opportunities for practice groups to continually meet and brush up on forming solution-focused questions and responses. The paradigm shift away from problem solving and toward solution building is a difficult one to make in our deficit focused culture, and an important part of the success of the Circle model. Using the *Interviewing for Solutions* (Dejong & Berg, 2008) text is a useful resource for all Circle facilitators to add to their libraries and use as a reference for developing and improving SFBT techniques.

B. Facilitator & Recorder Qualifications

The following list of qualifications is suggested for a facilitator, which can be adapted to your own organization's requirements for staff/independent contractors:

- bachelors degree or background in indigenous conflict resolution practices
- experience with traumatized and people suffering serious stress
- be certified by providing agency as competent to facilitate *Circles*
- good communication skills including listening, writing and speaking
- obtain any required state tax number or status for independent contractor if necessary
- ability to pass a state prison department security background check to gain access to prisons

The following list of qualifications is suggested for a recorder:
- good communication skills, including listening, writing and speaking
- legible handwriting
- be certified by providing agency to record *Circles*
- obtain any required state tax number or status for independent contractor if necessary
- ability to pass prison department security background check to gain access to prisons

C. Roles and Responsibilities for Facilitators and Recorders

The following is a list of suggested facilitator roles and responsibilities, which can be adapted to your own organization's needs:

- report to the Circle coordinator
- receive training in the Circle process
- complete security clearance with prison system
- complete any volunteer training program prison system provides
- interview applicants at prisons and explain program requirements and process

- convene *Circles* by: making reasonable efforts to contact all individuals the incarcerated person has requested participate e.g. internet and white pages searches to obtain contact information; provide information to prospective participants on nature of *Circle* process including sending a brochure; coordinate mutually agreeable scheduling of the *Circle*
- prepare all paperwork necessary to conduct the *Circle*
- coordinate the scheduling of the *Circle* with program coordinator, recorder, and any observers;
- conduct the three hour *Circle*
- disseminate and collect data collection instruments for all participants immediately following the *Circle*
- prepare draft *Circle* summary and transition plan within 3 working days of the *Circle*
- send draft *Circle* summary and transition plan to program coordinator for review who will return with any revisions within 24 hours
- revise and finalize *Circle* summary and transition plan within 24 hours of receiving it from coordinator
- disseminate copies of *Circle* summary and transition plan for all Circle participants and to the coordinator within 5 working days after conducting the Circle
- provide any immediate follow-up and/or referrals for *Circle* participants
- inquire regarding *Re-Circle* within 6 months of first *Circle* or sooner if necessary

The following is a list of suggested recorder roles and responsibilities, which can also be adapted to your own organization's needs.

- *Circle* recorders report to the program coordinator
- receive training in the *Circle* process and become certified by providing agency to record process
- complete security clearance with prison department
- complete any volunteer training program the prison department offers
- coordinate *Circle* scheduling with coordinator and assigned facilitators
- obtain all necessary supplies to conduct *Circle* e.g. pens, easel paper, tissues etc.;
- perform recording of three hour *Circle*

- assist in the dissemination and collection of data collection instruments for all participants immediately following the *Circle*
- perform de-brief with *Circle* facilitator
- notify coordinator of any significant issues or events that require immediate attention e.g. concerns regarding unexpected events with relationship to *Circle* program

II. Other Options: *Modified Circles* for Reentry and Transition Planning

The Modified Circle is a positive alternative for incarcerated people without any loved ones willing or able to attend a Circle on their behalf in prison (Walker, 2009). A Modified Circle is an especially good alternative if loved ones are estranged, and not willing to participate.

The Modified Circle addresses reconciliation and making a reentry plan, just as the full circle process does, but which requires at least one loved one to participate. When there are no loved ones able or willing to participate, the Modified Circle is an alternative with other incarcerated friends sitting in the Circle.

Providing an alternative recognizes that the imprisoned person's desire for a Circle is positive, and supports that choice. There are incarcerated people who have completely estranged their families and who have no positive support outside of prison. The Modified Circle can assist them in finding ways to reconcile and make an effective plan for reentry. Not providing any alternative when there are no loved ones available to attend can be discouraging to an incarcerated person. While the Modified Circle is not as rich and robust as a full Circle with loved ones participating, it can have a positive impact.

As discussed previously reconciliation for purposes of this process does not require repaired and restored relationships. While repaired relationships are a wonderful result of the Circles, there are lesser degrees of reconciliation that can assist both incarcerated people and others not attending a Circle.

An imprisoned person can reconcile within herself the effects that her behavior and incarceration has had on her and on others. She can make a plan for how to address her behavior, and how to make amends for it, with a group of incarcerated supporters. Communication with the people harmed is not necessary for the incarcerated person to work towards repairing harm. People who have been harmed do not need personal information about what the imprisoned person is doing to repair the harm for the incarcerated person to directly benefit.

The incarcerated person who decides to "walk the talk," that is to be law abiding, "clean and sober," employed, and independent financially, as a way to work toward repairing the harm she has caused, will increase her self-efficacy. Her work to repair the harm helps her deal with her shame and self-guilt. People harmed, who do not know about the incarcerated person's efforts, can indirectly benefit. Whenever another person is implementing positive actions, there are indirect benefits to others.

The formerly incarcerated person, who is law abiding, clean and sober, and working, brings indirect benefits to others in the community. She is no longer a drain on the community. Her criminal acts are no longer harming people, and the community is no longer paying for her incarceration. Instead she is contributing and promoting the welfare of others in important ways including paying taxes, being a good role model for others by taking responsibility for her life and future, and her other efforts toward repairing the harm.

Often the Modified Circle can give incarcerated people who are not sure they want to ask their loved ones to participate in a Circle, the opportunity to experience what the process is like and later apply for a full Circle. This has been the case for over 20 incarcerated people in Hawai'i. They had Modified Circles first then decided they wanted a full Circle and invited their loved ones to attend.

The Modified Circles follow the same agenda as the full Circle process, which includes loved ones. The Modified Circle instead is attended by other incarcerated supporters. Because loved ones are not participating, the reconciliation stage is much less emotional and more hypothetical with participants imagining how loved ones were affected, and what the incarcerated person might do to repair any harm. This makes the Modified Circle about an hour long, which is two-thirds less time than what a full Circle usually takes.

The Modified Circle Summary and Transition Plan is only provided to the incarcerated person and ideally the prison staff person who would participate. The Summary and Plan is not provided to the incarcerated people who participate in supporting the person having the Circle.

People who have had Modified Circles in Hawai'i have gained support from loved ones. One man who decided to address reconciliation with a former girlfriend's grandmother, gained back a relationship with his mother. The girlfriend's grandmother had read the kind and grateful letter he wrote her to his mother and days afterwards his mother contacted him for the first time in prison. He eventually gained the support of his mother when he was furloughed from prison about six months later (Walker, 2009).

III. Outcomes & Evaluation

A. Results of the Hawai'i Circle Program

Since 2005 a total of 66 full Huikahi Circles have been provided including four follow-up re-Circles. A total of 62 incarcerated people, 1 juvenile man, 46 adult men (one man was part of a couple that had a Circle in Finland) and 21 women, have had Circles (4 people have had Re-Circles). Over 340 people (family, friends, prison staff and/or counselors with treatment providers, and incarcerated individuals) have participated in the Circles.

Following each Circle, participants fill out surveys about their experience. One hundred percent (100%) of all 340 participants to date have reported that the Circle they participated in was a positive experience. Participant satisfaction and healing is a main outcome of the program.

In addition to the full 66 Huikahi Circles, 53 Modified Restorative Circles (22 for incarcerated women and 30 for men) have been provided in Hawai'i. One re-Circle was also provided in a California jail. The Modified Circles developed as an alternative for people whose loved ones were unable or unwilling to attend a full Circle in a prison (Walker, 2009) and currently in Hawai'i are only provided as part of a 12 week solution-focused & restorative justice training program (Walker & Sakai, 2006). Surveys from the Modified Circles also show 100% satisfaction of all participants.

The measure of recidivism is a critical factor in the evaluation of a reentry program. Methodology for determining recidivism rates varies. It is important to determine how and why you are measuring recidivism as applied. Funders often make their determinations of which organizations to support based on the evaluation plans for the intervention, and the potential to contribute to evidence based practices. A suggested way to develop an empirically sound evaluation method for your program is to partner with a local university who often can provide in-kind services and partner on grant writing.

While the samples are too small at this point in time to make clear judgments about whether the Circle process in Hawai'i prevents repeat crime, the percentages are promising. A total of 23 people who have had Circles, and have been out of prison for two years or more, have been studied to date. Ten of the 23 have been out of prison for three years or more. Out of the 23, 16 people (14 men and 2 women) have remained out of prison without any new known charges against them. Seven men are back in prison either for new arrests, new charges, or violations of parole. Approximately 70 percent have not been in contact with the criminal justice system and the remaining 30 percent have either been charged or convicted of new crimes, or violated the terms of their parole, and are back in prison.

Although the sample size of the Huikahi project is small, and reviewed subjects were out of prison for only two years, the 30 percent recidivism rate is significantly less than Hawai'i's overall 54.7 percent recidivism rate for formerly incarcerated people. Because of a lack of resources this project has been unable to provide necessary follow-up contacts and re-Circles. In light of the limited services provided, however, the project's preliminary recidivism rate remains promising, but evidence that the Circles prevent repeat crime is inconclusive at this time. What does remain solid is that loved ones report 100% satisfaction with the Circles even in cases where there is re-incarceration after Circles have been held (Walker & Greening, 2010). This indicator of healing is significant and should justify the intervention for communities interested in healthy residents.

B. Examining Overlooked Outcomes

While grant writing and other reasons require measuring outcomes in terms of contacts made and recidivism rates, other outcomes are equally as important to measure. In particular it has been important for the Hawai'i program to measure the value of the process to participants, even when the incarcerated person returns to the criminal justice system as a result of a parole/probation violation or new arrest. Parents and guardians continue to attest to the value of the Circle process, even in cases when the incarcerated person has relapsed and is back in prison.

The story of Marta, an aunt who raised her nephew who became re-incarcerated about a year after his Circle, demonstrates how the process increases social capital for families and children benefit as a result (Walker & Greening, 2010). As a result of the Circle, Marta met her nephew's girlfriend and she and the couple's children moved in with Auntie Marta, a former police sergeant. When Marta's nephew relapsed and went back to prison after the Circle (about a year after his release), the children and girlfriend continued living with Marta. She has provided important support to the young family ever since.

Another mother, who along with her 13 and 15 year old daughters, attended a 2005 Circle for their father who has since relapsed. The mother reflected on the Circle's value for her daughters who were 21 and 18 when she wrote this in 2010:

> My relationship with my children was strengthened. They knew I loved them dearly and would not turn my back on them, they knew I put them first. As of today, my children are aware of [their father's] vicious addiction, and the tragic outcomes. They have the knowledge to make suitable decisions for their upcoming adult lives, and practice in helping themselves to make better and positive decisions.

A mother of a woman who had a Circle and relapsed within only weeks after her release, describes how the process helped her and her grandchildren, who she has been raising for years:

> [It] helped my grandchildren get their frustrations out and direct their concern to their mother. It gave them a better understanding of all the hurt, guilt and confusion they had been dealing with for so long with their mother. Their outlook on how they tried to be supportive of their mother isn't so heavy on their lives now. They realize that it isn't their fault or responsibility to help their mother deal with all the problems that she brings upon herself. If she doesn't want to make the change or even make an effort to improve her situation, that they shouldn't carry the weight on their shoulders because she failed!

IV. Challenges with Providing the Program & Importance of Prison Leadership

The importance of working to maintain a good relationship with prison staff and administration cannot be overstated. The prison administration is vital to providing the program in the facilities. Working with them is as important as providing the Circles. The same skills used in communication with the incarcerated people can be used with prison staff and always remembering: "Everyone does the best they can with the knowledge that they have." Unless there are serious ethical infractions, judging and blaming prison staff will not further the program goals even when there are difficulties.

We believe the best way to convince prison staff that the Circle process is valuable is to invite them to observe a Circle. If they cannot be convinced that the Circles are a positive intervention for prisons, the process can be held outside of prison. The Circles can be conducted at the time of release, and provide support necessary for criminal desistance and a law abiding life.

One of the 66 Circles provided with loved ones was held at a church, and another was held at a formerly incarcerated person's mother's home.

Prison administrative challenges to providing the program can be overcome with "committed leadership" by prison staff:

> Circles also face two challenges from prison staff. First, the notion of empowering inmates in any way presents a challenge to some staff. In particular, the Circles require that inmates develop life plans without direction from staff. Skeptical staff may have difficulty with this, as it may be perceived as encroaching on their realm of responsibility. Second, Circles may be perceived to increase the workload of staff. Although the facilitator does most of the work, some things only prison staff can do, such as arrange space, obtain movement passes, and clear outside participants through security. Some staff feel overburdened with work, and fail to see the higher rehabilitative value of the Circles. These kinds of issues can be resolved by committed leadership within the prison. (Walker, Sakai & Brady, 2006).

In addition to claiming it requires unavailable resources to provide rehabilitation programs, prisons can also easily stop programs by claiming that they present unreasonable security risks. Constantly communicating with prison administration, state legislators, and the judiciary are ways to overcome barriers to providing the program.

Experience with justice leaders in Hawai'i shows the process is appreciated. In 2007 the Hawai'i parole board chief commented at a state legislative hearing that the incarcerated people who had the Circles and appeared before him "were transformed." He made this statement in support of a law to pilot the program, which unfortunately former Hawai'i governor Linda Lingle did not fund. An experienced deputy public defender also indicated that the Summary and Transition Plans for incarcerated people are an excellent resource for appearing before the parole board because they show exactly how all essential needs can be met.

David Wexler, co-founder of *therapeutic jurisprudence*, which is the basis for *problem solving courts* popular in the United States and other countries, was motivated to develop a correctional process for people to prepare for parole hearings based on what he learned of the Circle process (Wexler, 2011). Additionally, many Hawai'i state trial judges and appellate court justices have complimented the restorative justice work applied to corrections.

Applying for a Circle could also be part of a sentencing order imposed by a judge, just like restitution, fines, and probation are imposed. Many incarcerated, paroled, and people put on probation might want to have a Circle after learning about its benefits from an interview. If they did not want a Circle, one would not have to be held. This would take educating judges on the process and making them knowledgeable of the Circles' value for incarcerated people and their loved ones. With more information on the benefits of restorative justice and restorative practices, more judges will come to understand it, and hopefully, encourage people to consider these kinds of interventions.

V. Conclusion

Correction costs in the United States are unsustainable, and even if they were, we would have a scary society and unsafe communities if we continue on the current path of massive imprisonment. If we stay on this path the U.S. Department of Justice once reported that: "one out of every 15 people (6.6%) in the United States will serve time in a prison during their lifetime"[19] (USDOJ, 2011).

Correction programs and prisons need to work for rehabilitation, and not dehumanizing and further criminalizing people. Most incarcerated people eventually return to the community, and even for those who are never released, it is dangerous for communities, for other imprisoned people, and for the people who work in prisons, to ignore rehabilitation.

Research on the Circle process shows it is fairly easy to implement and a promising intervention for reducing repeat crime. Additionally, the process helps families heal and benefit even when there is repeat crime after a Circle. A mother describes how a Circle helped her family even after her daughter elapsed and went back to prison. She explains that despite the re-incarcerated of her daughter after the Circle, the process helped her, and her grandchildren, who she is raising:

> They don't let their mother's choices affect them where it makes them feel hurt or depressed anymore. They know she's an adult and that she needs to grow up and get with the program and whether she does or not they still respect her as their mother. They don't hesitate to tell her how much they love and care about her. So it was all good for all of us to get things off of our chest! . . . You just can't help someone who chooses to do her own thing, even though her choices have only gotten her deeper in trouble! There's only so much one can do to help her and she's taken all of us for granted for too long. Now she has to paddle her own canoe alone, because we need to go on with our lives putting one foot in front of the other and no more back stepping for us. It's no fun there and all of us just want to be happy and get on with living our lives in the light!

These reentry and transition planning Circles help families deal with guilt, shame, and other painful emotions when a loved one is imprisoned. The Circles also help incarcerated people see that they have support who can help them "paddle their canoes." The Circles engage all, and shine more light into lives of all participants, including prison staff. Circles can help rehabilitate incarcerated people, heal families, and transform prison cultures.

---

[19] The DOJ Bureau of Statistics no longer posts this statement, but the authors read it there, which others also cite. See: http://answers.google.com/answers/threadview/id/545987.html.

References

Baer,D., Bhati, A., Brooks, L., Castro, J., La Vigne, N., Mallik-Kane, K., Naser, R., Osborne, J., Roman, C., Rossman, S., Solomon, A., Visher, C., & Winterfield, L., 2006. Understanding the Challenges of Prisoner Reentry: Research Findings from the Urban Institute's Prisoner Reentry Portfolio, *Urban Institute*, Washington D.C., p. 8.

Bazemore, G., & Maruna, S., 2009. Restorative Justice in the Reentry Context: Building New Theory and Expanding the Evidence Base. *Victims and Offenders.* 4(4):375-384.

Berg, I.K. (undated). Retrieved August 4, 2011 from: http://www.sfbta.org/about_sfbt.html

Berg, I.K. & de Shazer, S., 1993. Making Numbers Talk: Language in Therapy. In S. Friedman (ed.), *The new language of change: Constructive collaboration in psychotherapy.* New York: Guilford Press.

Brantley, J., 2007. *Calming your anxious mind: How mindfulness & compassion can free you from anxiety, fear & panic.* Oakland, CA: New Harbinger Publications.

Clark, H., (1996) *Using Language.* Cambridge, UK: Cambridge University Press

Dejong, P., & Berg. I., (2008). *Interviewing for Solutions.* Pacific Grove, CA: Brooks/Cole.

Dweck, C., 2006. *Mindset: The New Psychology of Success.* NY: Random House.

Eglash, A., 1977. "Beyond restitution: Creative restitution." In J.Hudson and B.Galaway (eds). *Restitution in criminal justice.* Lexington, MA:Lexington Books.

Ellis, A., 1991. *Reason and Emotion in Psychotherapy.* NY: Carol Publishing Group.

Furman, B., & Walker, L. 2011. Apology & Forgiveness interactive web program. Retrieved September 1, 2011 from: http://www.apologyletter.org/

Sacks, H. & Garfinkel, H. 1970. "On formal structures of practical action," in J.C. McKinney and E.A. Tiryakian (eds.), Theoretical Sociology, Appleton-Century-Crofts, New York, 1970, pp. 338–366. Reprinted in H. Garfinkel, ed., (1986) Ethnomethodological Studies of Work, 160-193.

Green, L., 2010. A Short History of the Compassionate Listening Project. Accessed February 28, 2011 from: http://www.compassionatelistening.org/about/history

Hairston, C.F., 2007. Focus on Children with Incarcerated Parents: An Overview of the Research Literature, Accessed January 4, 2011 www.aecf.org/childrenofincarcerated.aspx

Hall, D. (2011). *Criminal Law and Procedure.* NY: West Legal Studies Series.

Hawai'i State Legislature, 2010. Senate Concurrent Resolution 192 S.D.1, REQUESTING THE DEPARTMENT OF PUBLIC SAFETY TO FACILITATE THE DELIVERY OF THE HUIKAHI RESTORATIVE CIRCLES PROGRAM IN HAWAI'I CORRECTIONAL FACILITIES.

Healey, K., 1999. Case Management in the Criminal Justice System, United States, *National Institute of Justice.*

Hogg, M. & Cooper, J., 2003. *Sage Handbook of Social Psychology.* Thousand Oaks, CA: Sage Publications Inc.

Howerton, A., Burnett, R., Byng, R., & Campbell, J., 2009. The Consolations of Going Back to Prison: What 'Revolving Door' Prisoners Think of Their Prospects, *Journal of Offender Rehabilitation*, 48(5): 439—461.

Hwoschinsky, C., 2001. *Listening with the heart: A guide for compassionate listening.* Indianola, Washington:The Compassionate Listening Project.

Interagency Council on Intermediate Sanctions 2010. State of Hawai'i. Accessed April 10, 2011 from: http://Hawai'i.gov/icis/documents/

Iverson, C., 2002. Solution Focused Brief Therapy. *Advances in Psychiatric Treatment, Vol. 8.* Accessed March 19, 2011 from: http://uqu.edu.sa/files2/tiny_mce/plugins/filemanager/files/4140225/Solution-focused%20brief%20therapy.pdf

Jenkins, A., 1990. *Invitations to Responsibility: The therapeutic engagement of men who are violent and abusive.* Adelaide, South Australia: Dulwich Centre Publications.

Jordan, M., 2011. About.com Quotations. Accessed February 3, 2011 http:quotations.about.com/od/stillmorefamouspeople/a/MichaelJordan1.htm

Langer, E., 1989. *Mindfulness.* Reading, MA: Addison-Wesley Publishing Co, Inc.

Lee, M.Y., Sebold, J. & Uken, A., 2003. *Solution-Focused Treatment of Domestic Violence Offenders: Accountability for Change.* NY: Oxford.

Kabat-Zinn, J., 1994. *Wherever You Go There You Are.* NY: Hyperion.

Maruna, S. 2001. *Making Good: How Ex-Convicts Reform and Rebuild Their Lives.* Washington, DC: American Psychological Association Books.

Maruna, S., LeBel, T. & Lanier, C., 2004. "Generativity Behind Bars: Some 'Redemptive Truth' about Prison Society" (pp.131-152) in E. de St. Aubin, D. McAdams & T. Kim (Eds.) The Generative Society. Washington, DC: American Psychological Association.

Mills, L., 1998. *Heart of intimate abuse: New interventions in child welfare, criminal justice, and health settings.* NY: Springer.

Nouwen, H., 1996. *Bread for the Journey: A Daybook of Wisdom and Faith.* NY: HarperOne.

Rose, D. & Clear, T., 2002. Incarceration, Reentry, and Social Capital: Social Networks in the Balance, *From Prison to Home: The Effect of Incarceration and Reentry on Children, Families, and Communities.* Accessed January 13, 2011 http://aspe.hhs.gov/hsp/prison2home02/Rose.htm

Rumgay, J., 2004. Scripts for safer survival: Pathways out of female crime. *The Howard Journal,* 43(4), 405–419.

Schwartz, S. & Boodell, D., 2009. *Dreams from the Monster Factory.* NY: Scribner.

Seligman, M., 2006. *Learned Optimism: How to Change Your Mind and Your Life.* NY: Vintage.

Sherman, L., & Stang, H., *The Evidence,* The Smith Institute, Somerset House, London. Accessed August 15, 2011 from: http://www.smith-institute.org.uk/file/ RestorativeJusticeTheEvidenceFullreport.pdf

Shover, N., 1996. *The Great Pretenders: Pursuits and Careers of Persistent Thieves.* Boulder, Colorado: Westview Press.

Smock, S., Bavelas, J., Froerer, A., Korman, H., & De Jong, P. 2010. *Are SFBT and CBT really different? Using Microanalysis to Compare What Therapists Do,* EBTA/SFBTA Conference Presentation, Malmo, Sweden.

Tavris, C. & Aronson, E. 2007. *Mistakes Were Made (but not by me): Why We Justify Foolish Beliefs, Bad Decisions, and Hurtful Acts.* NY: Houghton Mifflin Harcourt.

The Stockholm Prize in Criminology, 2006. Accessed April 10, 2011 from: http:// www.criminologyprize.com/extra/pod/?id=24&module_instance=3&action=pod_show&navid=24

Trepper, T., McCollum, E., De Jong, P., Korman, H., Gingerich, W., & Franklin, C., 2010. Solution Focused Therapy Treatment Manual for Working with Individuals, *Research Committee of the Solution Focused Brief Therapy Association.* Accessed July 10, 2011 from: http://www.sfbta.org/research

Travis, J., 2005. *But They All Come Back: Facing the Challenges of Prisoner Reentry.* Washington DC:Urban Institute.

United States, Bureau of Justice Statistics, 2002. Accessed March 19, 2011 from: http:// bjs.ojp.usdoj.gov/index.cfm?ty=pbdetail&iid=1134

USDOJ, U.S. Department of Justice, National Archive of Criminal Justice Data, Retrieved on September 1, 2011 from: http://www.icpsr.umich.edu/cgi-bin/NACJD/bjspubs#piusp01

Walker, L., 2010. Huikahi Restorative Circles: Group Process for Self-Directed Reentry Planning and Family Healing, *European Journal of Probation,* Walker, October 2010, 2:2, p. 76-95. Accessed July 2, 2011 from: http://www.ejprob.ro/index.pl/ huikahi_restorative_circlesgroup_process_for_self-directed_reentry_planning_and_family_healing

Walker, L., 2009. Modified Restorative Circles: A Reintegration Group Planning Process That Promotes Desistance, *Contemporary Justice Review,* Vol. 12, No. 4, 419-431

Walker, L., 2005. E Makua Ana, Youth Circles: A Transition Planning Process for Youth Exiting Foster Care, *VOMA Connections,* No. 21, Fall.

Walker, L. & Sakai, T., 2006. A Gift of Listening for Hawaii Inmates, *Corrections Today,* December.

Walker, L., Sakai, T. & Brady, K., 2006. Restorative Circles: A Reentry Planning Process for Inmates, *Federal Probation Journal,* June 2006, Vol. 70, No. 1. Accessed July 3, 2010 from: http://www.uscourts.gov/uscourts/FederalCourts/PPS/Fedprob/2006-06/circles.html

Walker, L. & Greening, R., 2010. Huikahi Restorative Circles: A Public Health Approach for Reentry Planning, *Federal Probation Journal,* 74(1*).* Accessed August 15, 2011 from: http://www.uscourts.gov/uscourts/FederalCourts/PPS/Fedprob/2010-06/06_restorative_circles.html

Wexler, D., 2011. Retooling Reintegration: A Reentry Moot Court, *Chapman Journal of Criminal Justice,* Vol. 2 No.1. 191-202.

Zehr, H., 1990. *Changing Lenses.* Scottsdale. PA: Good Books.

Zimbardo, P., 2007. *The Lucifer Effect: How Good People Turn Evil.* NY: Random House.

The Authors

Lorenn Walker, JD, MPH, is a Hawai'i based health educator who develops, implements and evaluates interventions promoting peaceful communities and well-being for individuals. She is a former Hawai'i State Deputy Attorney General who defended state agencies and prosecuted individuals. She later represented and defended youth and adults in criminal and child protection cases. She received her juris doctorate at Northeastern University School of Law and her masters degree in health education from the School of Public Health, University of Hawai'i at Manoa. She is the author of numerous publications: http://www.lorennwalker.com/ Her email addresses are: lorenn@hawaii.edu & lorenn@hawaii.rr.com

Rebecca Greening, JD, is a Juvenile Court Public Defender in Boston. She previously clerked with Lorenn Walker and the Hawai'i Friends of Justice & Civic Education assisting in the provision of reentry circles in Hawai'i prisons. She also clerked with the Middlesex Probate & Family Court and The Wilmer Hale Legal Services Center. She holds a bachelor of science in social work from New York University and received her juris doctorate from Northeastern University School of Law. Her advocacy work seeks to incorporate restorative justice approaches in both civil and criminal contexts.

APPENDIX

Appendix A - Circle Application Form

Huikahi Referral Form Fax to **637-1284** Phone for information: 637-2385	

Case manager/contact name:	Case manager/contact phone: Cell Ph: Fax:

Incarcerated Person's Name:	Last four numbers Social Security:	Expected release date:

(protected & only used for research):

Age:	Highest level of education:	Last school attended:	Offense & date imprisoned for:

Date desired for Huikahi?:	Date referred:

Has Huikahi been explained to client? YES NO   First referral? YES NO   Hawaiian ancestry? YES NO

Additional comments:

Name of primary person harmed:	Age:	Phone:

NAMES OF POTENTIAL SUPPORTERS—FAMILY & FRIENDS	RELATIONSHIP	PHONE
	Father	
	Mother	

NAMES OF PROFESSIONALS / OTHERS	AGENCY	PHONE
	Case Manager	
	Counselor	

After this application is received a facilitator will schedule an interview with the applicant. Please call at (808) 637-2385 if you do not hear from us within two weeks. Mahalo.

Appendix B - Circle Brochure

(exterior)

[Name of reentry & transition planning] Circles:

Creating a Positive Future

A Program for Confined and Imprisoned People to Heal, Make Amends with Loved Ones and Others Harmed by Past Behavior & Plan for a Successful Life

[Names and contact information of individuals working with organization providing Circles]

Name and website of organization providing Circle
Date brochure prepared

[Name of reentry & transition planning process] circle with your loved ones please contact your case manager, counselor or social worker and ask for an application.

Appendix B - Circle Brochure

(interior)

[Name] Circles are a group process based on public health learning principals for people in prison, work furlough or drug treatment programs to make plans for a successful life including making amends with family, friends, and others harmed by past behavior.

[Name] Circles are special meetings for you to meet with your 'ohana. A *Transition Plan* is developed at the Circle outlining what you **need** for a successful life; how you **want to live** differently compared to the past; and how you might **make amends**.

An interview takes place with a facilitator who will contact your loved ones about scheduling a **circle.**

You choose whom to invite and we talk personally with all those invited before your **[name of process]** group meeting. A representative from the facility you are leaving attends each **Circle.** Other resource people, who might be able to help you in the community, may also be invited to attend your **Circle.**

Circles are a positive planning process that focus on how people leaving confinement can transition and create positive lives.

The **solution-focused** approach guides the **Circle** process where your strengths and resources are considered. **Follow-up Circle** groups are held. Each group is unique and the number of your follow-up **Circles** depends on each person. Other restorative meetings may also be held with people who did not attend the **Circle** if they agree to participate. **Making amends** is done by discussing how people were affected by your past behavior, and what can be done to repair the harm. An agreement to repair the harm is made at the Circle and is included in your Transition Plan. **Before a Circle** is held you decide what you want different for your future and how you want to open your **Circle**, i.e. a poem, prayer, song, words of inspiration, etc. **Circles each take about 3 hours** Contact your case manager, counselor, or social worker for more information and/or to request an application for a **Circle.**

Circle Agenda:

Welcome & Opening: You open **Circle.**

Introduction: Name & relationship of each participant to you.

Purpose & Guidelines: To assist you reconcile and plan for a successful transition back into the community. Participants speak one at a time & respect confidentiality.

You are asked: "What is something you are especially proud of that you have accomplished in prison?"

Strengths: Each person shares your strengths.

Reconciliation: You are asked: "Who was affected by your behavior? How were they affected?" Your 'ohana is asked: "How were you affected?" And "What might be done to repair the harm?" You are also asked if you can do whatever they want. Later you're asked: "How might you reconcile with people hurt who are not present today?"

Short Break

What do you want for your future: "How do you want your life to be different from the past?"

Group brainstorms resource options: housing, financial, continued learning, employment, transportation, documents, emotional & physical health.

Make a Transition Plan & list supporters & a timetable for completion.

Next Circle Date: Schedule date.

Circle Closing: Group compliments you & you say how the Circle process was for you; everyone completes an evaluation.

Breaking of Bread: After each **Circle** there is an informal gathering with simple refreshments if prison allows food.

Appendix C - Circle Summary & Transition Plan

[name of program e.g. *Huikahi* in Hawai'i] Circle Summary & Transition Plan
For [Incarcerated Person's (IP) name]

DATE OF CIRCLE: [date]   **LOCATION OF CIRCLE**: [name & location of prison]

PURPOSE: To assist [Incarcerated Person's (IP) name] to make amends for her past behavior and imprisonment, and to develop a transition plan for returning to the community after serving time at [name of prison].

Accomplishments that [IP's name] is most proud of during her/his time at [name of prison]:

[IP's name] STRENGTHS:

Takes responsibility for her/his life and working to make amends with those s/he hurt in past and by her incarceration

WAYS [IP's name] WANTS HER/HIS LIFE TO BE DIFFERENT THAT IT WAS IN THE PAST:

[IP's name] PLAN FOR SUCCESSFUL TRANSITION BACK INTO THE COMMUNITY

THINGS TO DO	BY WHOM	DATE TO BE COMPLETED BY
1. **RECONCILIATION – what [IP's name] will do to repair the harm to her/his loved ones for her/his past behavior & incarceration:** **For [name loved one e.g. "Brother, Eric, Mother, Child Melissa, etc.** [describe what IP is going to do e.g. "stay clean and sober"] **RECONCILIATION WITH UNRELATED People:** [describe what IP is going to do e.g. "stay clean and sober"]	[IP's name]	
2. **HOUSING** [list at least 3 different housing alternative]	[IP's name]	
3. **CONTINUED LEARNING/ EDUCATION:** [list everything IP is interested in learning about, doesn't have to be formal schooling]	[IP's name]	
4. **FINANCIAL & EMPLOYMENT:** [list how IP is going to get $ and find employment]	[IP's name]	
5. **DOCUMENTS Birth Certificate, Social Security card, Driver's License, State ID card, etc.:** [list how IP will obtain her necessary legal documents]	[IP's name]	

6. TRANSPORTATION:	[IP's name]	
7. PHYSICAL HEALTH: [list what IP plans to do to maintain or achieve good physical health]	[IP's name]	
8. EMOTIONAL HEALTH: [list what IP plans to do to maintain or achieve good emotion health]	[IP's name]	
9. SUPPORTERS: [list who IP can call on for support]		
10. Other: [list any other needs not previously addressed, e.g. apply for a divorce, determine legal custody of children, etc.]	[IP's name]	
11: FOLLOW UP CIRCLE DATE: [when does IP want a follow up Circle?]	[IP's name]	

Participants at the Circle [list all participants and their relationship to IP and any observers present]; [facilitator's name], and [recorder's name]

Anytime anyone believes additional Circles are needed or needs assistance, please call [facilitator and her/his phone number.

Thank for your participation in the Circle.

Appendix D - Facilitator's Agenda

Reentry & Transition Planning Circle
Facilitator's Agenda

1. Circle Opening

Incarcerated person [IP] opens Circle any way s/he chooses, i.e. makes a statement, recites a poem, prayer, (some people ask a loved one to say a prayer) sings a song, plays ukulele, chants, etc.

2. Introductions

"Thank you for coming. I am [facilitator's name] and I will be facilitating today's Circle. Please tell us your name and relationship with [incarcerated person's name]."

Start with Circle recorder, go around Circle starting with prison or program staff representative, who is seated to right of the facilitator and end with incarcerated person [IP] who is seated to the facilitator's left.

3. Purpose & Guidelines

"The purpose of this Circle is to help [IP's name] find ways for him/her to reconcile and make amends for his/her past behavior and to make a plan for a successful life and transition back into the community."

"We assume everyone will speak one at a time in the Circle and respect confidentiality." (Facilitator looks around to all the people in the Circle nodding her head up and down, seeking to obtain agreement from the participants).

4. Incarcerated Person's Proudest Accomplishment in Prison

Ask IP: "Please tell us what you are especially proud of that you have accomplished while you've been here in prison?"

5. Incarcerated Person's Strengths

If children/youth participating: "Before we go into [IP name's] strengths and what people like about her/him, one of her/his biggest strengths is sitting right here [look to IP's child]. Let's hear what the child's/children's strengths they are."

Begin with participant least attached to family or family sitting furthest away—prison staff or program staff person: "You've probably only just met [child's name] what strengths to you see? What do you like about [child's name]?"

End with the child asking: "Did they leave out anything great about you?"

If no children or youth are participating and after you have collected with the group lists as the IP's strengths. Ask prison or program staff representative first: "What are some of [IP's name] strengths?" Go around the Circle and end with IP asking, "Did they leave out any other strengths you have?"

6. Reconciliation phase of Circle: Can say "Another Strength [IP's name] has is taking responsibility" or "As [so and so] mentioned, another strength IP has is being accountable."

"[IP's name] is here today because s/he wants to find ways to reconcile for her/his past behavior and imprisonment. Her/his taking responsibility to make amends, to try and makes things right, and to make a plan for the future. This is another strength that s/he has."

"Let's begin with asking [IP's name]."

Ask IP:

"Who was affected in the past by your behavior?

"How were they affected?"

"What were you thinking at the time you did the harmful things?"

"What have you thought since then?"

Ask each loved one present starting with person sitting furthest away from IP:

"How were you affected by [IP's name] behavior and imprisonment?"

"What can [IP's name] do to try and repair the harm caused to you?"

As each person says what he or she would like IP to do go back to IP and ask: "Can you do that?" When the response is yes, good to ask IP: **"What gives you hope that you can do that?"**

Ask IP & group: "Are there any other related and unrelated people not here today that need to be considered for reconciliation?"

If yes, ask "How were they affected? What could [IP's name] do to try and make things right with them? Include whatever is suggested that the group agrees on.

Ask IP: "Do you have anything else you want to say right now?"

BREAK 5 – 10 MINUTES

7. Transition Planning stage of Circle:

"Now that you've made a reconciliation agreement, we can look at the other needs [IP's name] has for a successful transition from prison and find our what s/he wants for her/his future.

Ask IP: "What do you want to be different with your life from how it was in the past? What are your goals?" If IP says s/he wants to stay clean or crime free, ASK her or him again: "*What gives you hope you can do that?*"

8. Brainstorming Resources to meet Needs:

"Now we're going to generate lists of options and resources for [IP's name] to meet his/her needs to reach their goals. We want everyone here to put in their ideas. These are just possibilities—don't worry if they will work or not. We're only brainstorming. Any ideas are good. The more ideas the better."

"Let's start with housing. What are some of the options for [IP's name] for housing after he leaves prison?" Go around the Circle if people don't just start giving ideas—try to get a little something from everyone. We always list at least 3 housing alternatives and if the person is going on parole make clear it will be up to the parole board to agree on housing decisions.

Go though each area of needs: housing, continued learning/education, financial & employment, documents (birth certificate, social security card, state identification (ID), driver's license/driver's permit, medical cards, etc.), transportation, maintain or achieving physical health, emotional health in the same manner.

List her/his circle of supporters. Ask IP: "Who will you turn to when you need help?"

Discuss any other special topics—like childcare, setting up a behavioral contract for incarcerated people who will be returning to their parent's home, getting divorced or other legal issues.

Recorder collects all information under headings on large butcher paper taped on walls.

9. Timelines Established

For each need, e.g. housing, employment, transportation, etc., discussed in the Plan ask, "How can this be accomplished? What date will it be done by?" Be very concrete in making the transition plan —get dates for everything.

10. Follow-up re-Circle Date

Present to the group: "Follow up is important. Plans change and something work out differently from what we expected. When should we schedule a time to come back and see how this Plan went?" Set a specific date for the IP to call you or for you to contact the IP to schedule a re-Circle.

11. Circle Closing

Begin with the prison staff person and say: "We'll close this Circle by complementing [IP's name] on something new you heard or learned today about her/him, or something else you'd like them to know." Go around Circle

End Circle by asking IP, "How was this process for you? Is there anything you would like to say?"

12. Sign Circle Summary & Distribute Circle Evaluations

Thank participants for coming. Distribute the Summary and Surveys for everyone to sign and tell them you will mail them a copy.

13. Breaking of Bread & Informal Social Interaction of Circle Participants & Observers

Informal gathering of all participants and any observers with food and drinks (if allowed by prison)—give left over food and drinks to the family or prison guards if the family can't take it out of prison.

Appendix E - Sign In Sheet

[name of reentry & transition planning process] CIRCLE SIGN-IN SHEET

NAME: [Incarcerated Person's name]   **Date:** [date of Circle]

Thank you for coming to this [name of reentry and transition planning] Circle. We ask that you protect the privacy of the incarcerated person and Circle participants. By signing this you are saying that you understand and agree to respect the confidentiality of the Circle participants. Please fill in or correct any errors in your name, address. If your name is not listed, please print and sign your name, and provide your address and phone number.

NAME	RELATIONSHIP TO INCARCERATED PERSON	MAILING ADDRESS* (INCLUDE ZIP CODE) & PHONE NUMBER
Print: Sign:	Self	[prison address]
Print: Sign:		
Print: Sign:		
Print: Sign:		
Print: Sign:		
Print: Sign:		
Print: Sign:		

FACILITATOR: [name of facilitator]   **RECORDER:** [recorder's name]

*some people do not want others to know their address & phone, which is kept private

Appendix F - Example Circle Summary & Transition Plan

Huikahi Restorative Circle Summary & Transition Plan for Kathy Lee

DATE OF CIRCLE: January 5, 2011   **LOCATION:** Women's Community Correctional Facility, Oʻahu

PURPOSE: To assist Kathy to make amends with for her past behavior and imprisonment, and to develop a transition plan for returning to the community after serving time at Women's Community Correctional Facility (WCCC).

PROUDEST ACCOMPLISHMENTS WHILE INCARCERATED:

Completed drug treatment program; completed reentry course (earned tokens for benefits after release e.g. clothes, bus pass); took classes including anger management, cognitive restructuring, and parenting; participate regularly in NA/AA; completed restorative justice & solution focused problem solving course.

KATHY'S STRENGTHS: Her strengths include her four children and her granddaughter: 2 year old granddaughter Lani; 15 year old daughter Michelle; 18 year old daughter Jamie; 20 year old daughter Tess; and 23 year old daughter Nanci. Lani, Jamie and Tess could not attend the Circle but they, along with Kathy's parents, contributed their thoughts by telephone interview before the Circle.

Lani strengths (granddaughter 2 years old attended Circle):

Smiles
Laughs
Loving
Changed Tess' life around
Keeps the family going
Everything to Tess
Motivated Aunty Nanci to stay and hold house together
She's Kathy's life
Wonderful spirit
Has a lot of energy
She likes to play
Likes to make a mess
Likes to draw
Creative
Loves to catch the bus
Walks with Jamie to the store
Good company
Keeps Jamie occupied
She is a blessing
Free with feelings
Loving baby
Makes people smile

Continued Strengths of Lani:

Made her family happier
Energetic
Engaging
Intelligent
Disciplined enough to sit through almost 3 hour Circle!
She is loved tremendously by her family

Malia strengths (15 year daughter could not attend Circle):
Loves me
Buys me things
Talks to me every week on the phone
Takes me places when we're together
Has a beautiful smile
Takes good care of me and my sisters
Has a good sense of humor

Jamie strengths (18 year daughter could not attend Circle):
Loving
Has a loving family who adore her
Takes care Lani
Funny
Smart
Full spirited
Caring
Cheerful
Wants to work
Looking for jobs
Wants happiness in life
Strong
Has Tess' back
Humorous
Sticks with sisters thoughts ups and downs
Finds love in everything

Tess strengths (20 year old daughter attended Circle):
Kind
Persistent
Good mom
Saves $
Soft hearted
Respectful
Open-minded
Passionate
Proud mom
When her sisters need her help she's there
Not afraid to work hard
She's healthy

Tess' continued strengths:
Knows blood is thicker than water
Independent
Learns from her mistakes
Hard worker
Supports her child
Good parent
Helps me out
Gives Jamie bus money and for girl things
Generous
Shares
Can be funny
Hard worker
Works everyday Monday through Friday
Gets up early
Takes good care of Lani
Really loves Lani
Good sister

Nanci strengths (23 year old daughter attended Circle):
Hard worker
Works 2 jobs & goes to school
Takes care of her younger sisters
Very responsible including taking over home & helping younger sisters when mom went to prison
Provides her sisters in Hawai'I with cell phones and monitors their use (if they don't live up to their responsibly Nanci takes the phones away from them)
Self-disciplined
Helps others
Got loan to pay $3000 restitution & attorney fees for her mother
Saving $ and to buy a condo
Doing a good job in everything
Let's Jamie use her car to go to work
Takes Jamie all kind of places she needs to go
Helps Jamie with job interviews
Cruises and laughs with friends
Hard worker
Hard working student too
Good role model for sisters, mom and niece
Good with kids
She and Tess have both taken a lot of mom's prior responsibilities over since her incarceration
Cares about other people
Puts her own interests aside for others
A strong support in her sister's lives
Very soft hearted
Has good friends whose families have positively influenced her
She is wise & chooses good friends
Inspirational person for anyone

Kathy's other strengths that her mother Mrs. Lee identified by telephone interview:
Good heart
Will help anybody who asks for help
Has a lot of friends
Friendly
Her friends are crazy about her
Knows what she needs to do to make it
Smart girl
Can figure out things
Beautiful smile
Great conversationalist
Very emotional
Loves her kids
Loves people
Hard worker when she can get a job
Very clean person
Kind hearted
Takes very good care of herself

Kathy's other strengths that her father Mr. Lee identified by telephone:
Good person
Helpful to others
Give you the shirt off her back
Outgoing
Gets along with others well
Confident
Funny
A lot of friends
Makes friends easily
Pretty good hard worker

Kathy's other strengths people in Circle identified:
Self-sufficient
There for her kids
Cared for Lani
Compassionate
Helped Tess learn how to care for Lani
Taught daughters to be independent
Loves her kids
Other kids always welcome in her home
Has a loving family
Taught her girls to care about other people & to work hard
Very hard worker—4 jobs one time previously
Has accomplished a lot in prison
Used prison to improve herself & learn about herself
Doesn't' feel sorry for her self
Finds ways to make family stronger
Nanci is a mirror image of her
Core of family even in prison

Kathy's continued strengths:
Instilled idea of family & good values in children
Good listener
People feel comfortable talking to her
Trust worthy person
Humble
Taught daughters how to be self-sufficient and how to respect people
Has good manners
Always there for her daughters
Loving
Hard worker
Works 7 days a week
Loves everyone
Cooks good
Helps Jamie out with things important to her
Jamie can always talk to her
Remorseful for past hurtful behavior
Takes responsibility & wants to make amends

HOW KATHY WANTS HER LIFE TO BE DIFFERENT IN THE FUTURE THAN IT HAS BEEN IN THE PAST (her goals):

Always remember lessons she has learned in life including the behavior that brought her to prison and to get a job, continue working hard, and caring for her children and grandchildren.

THINGS TO DO	BY WHOM	COMPLETION DATE
1. RECONCILIATION WITH RELATED LOVED ONES PRESENT AT CIRCLE: What Kathy will do to work to repair the harm for her past behavior & incarceration: Nanci & Tess asked that she stay out of any romantic relationship with their father—divorce him; get out of prison ASAP and when she is released spend time with them and Lani; she can write to their father but no "interpersonal/romantic relationship" will occur; don't go back to jail—learn from her behavior. She also wants to write each of her daughters an apology letter (she already asked each how they were affected and they shared what they need for her to do to repair the harm). Attached is an apology letter form she can refer to. **RECONCILIATION WITH LOVED ONES NOT PRESENT AT CIRCLE:**	Kathy	She is doing what she can to get released and what is possible while incarcerated. She will do other things not possible in prison after she is released. Her plans to file for a divorce are addressed in the "other" section of this plan. She will mail the apology letters to her daughters by January 31.
For daughter Malia: Be a mother – take care of children, be there for us & provide for our emotional and physical needs Stay clean and sober Go to church **For daughter Jamie:** Come out of jail Not clean houses anymore if she is going to steal from owners Don't break any more laws Don't do anything she could get arrested for Want her to stop having relationship with dad Don't go back to dad **For her Mother:** Stay busy Get a job that keeps her busy Focus on her job Focus on maintaining good spirit Get some grieving counseling or join a group for grieving people See a counselor Be in her kids' lives more – communicate with them regularly Get herself together so Malia can come to Hawai'i and spend summer and holidays with her and her sisters **For her Father:** Get her life in order Straighter her life out Do things parents need to do Get herself together Malia is graduating from school soon & needs her	Kathy	Doing what's possible for everyone while incarcerated and will do other things not possible in prison after her release.

THINGS TO DO	BY WHOM	COMPLETION DATE
RECONCILIATION WITH OTHERS HARMED NOT AT CIRCLE: Henderson family--Kathy will write a letter to Mrs. Henderson expressing her sincere apology and can follow the www.apologyletter.org format that Lorenn will attach to the Plan when sent to Kathy. Earl Larson her prison counselor will review the letter and sign a statement on it that he reviewed it and that Kathy seems sincere. Kathy will mail the letter to Lorenn who will try and locate Mrs. Henderson's address. If Lorenn obtains the address she will send Kathy's letter along with a cover letter explaining Kathy participated in a Circle and wanted to formally apologize. **For the community at large:** she will stay clean **2. HOUSING (Kathy understands that all her plans including housing must be approved by the parole board)** 1. Clean and sober house – getting a list from Liz to write to for info on vacancies and Lorenn will ask for referrals and advice on which places are best run with residents motivated and living clean lives 2.TJ Mahoney Program – Kathy will make request to ask her prison case manager for information on referral & Lorenn asked Lorraine Robinson about program and found out it is very structured for a full 6 mos—it is like being in a correctional work furlough program—not clear this is what Kathy is looking for as she wants to work, save money and get her children back and a lot of structure might not fit with her needs/desires 3. Live with her daughters on O'ahu	Kathy, Earl & Lorenn Kathy, Liz & Lorenn	Kathy will write letter within one week of receiving the Plan and give it to Earl to review within 2 days of writing letter and mail it to Lorenn with Earl's approval signature on it within 2 days of his review-- she has stamps and envelop. Liz will send Kathy a list of clean and sober houses and also send her a draft letter and make copies of it to write the house re: vacancies when she anticipates being released. She will write and mail the letters by January 14; Lorenn will try and get referral information on the good clean and sober houses and get it to Kathy before she goes to parole board January 20; Lorenn obtained information as noted on TJ program (may be too structured to fit Kathy's needs but if she is interested she should pursue with her case manager for a referral).

THINGS TO DO	BY WHOM	COMPLETION DATE
3. CONTINUED LEARNING/EDUCATION: She loves learning from NA/AA and learning more about sobriety and improving life quality and wants to continue this	Kathy	Ongoing
Learn more about commuters – likes business education – with Liz's help Kathy will write to various community colleges for information on programs to find one to work towards getting into	Kathy	Write colleges by Wednesday January 12
4. FINANCIAL & EMPLOYMENT Apply for Jewish Federation scholarship to help her with housing will write to them and request information	Kathy	Write by January 14
Apply for General Assistance from state department of human services which she will be eligible for for about 2 months after prison release	Kathy	Apply DHS when released or as soon as possible before release if allowed
Look for employment with Worknet, Work Links & Life Styles programs for help– use list Dawn gave her to find job	Kathy	Begin looking for work ASAP after release – ask Chaz about Life Styles program support after release
5. DOCUMENNTS: Birth certificate, social security card, driver's license, state ID, etc. Kathy's Mom believes she has her birth certificate and social security and expired driver's license and will send them by registered postal service to: Dawn Slaten, Esq. P.O. Box 16 Aiea, HI 96701 Dawn will keep them and give them to Kathy	Kathy, Mom & Dawn	Mrs. King (Mom) will look for the documents ASAP and mail to Dawn's address after the January 20 parole board hearing and Dawn will provide Kathy when released
6. TRANSPORTATION Bus and will ask Chaz about tokens for bus	Kathy	Ask Chaz ASAP and use bus after release

THINGS TO DO	BY WHOM	COMPLETION DATE
7. PHYSICAL HEALTH: Drink at least 8 cups of water daily – 4 with lunch and 4 with dinner and as needed in between Walk 1 hour daily for aerobic – mornings before work Eat real good – stay off carbs, don't eat until full – allow self to be a little hungry when she stops eating – eat chicken, fish, turkey, vegetables (which she loves), apples and fruit	Kathy	Ongoing in prison as possible and continue or being on release
8. EMOTIONAL HEALTH Daily devotionals every morning for 30 minutes including read Bible, prayers, and read self-help books Practice positive self talk upon waking and every morning think of at least one thing to be grateful for Stay around positive people – stay connected to her family—those in California by internet which is free in public libraries and can also look into Skyping with them as she gains computer access after release. Connect with daughters in Hawai'I daily Go to church 1x a week – will get list of New Hope Church locations from Liz to find churches to attend	Kathy Kathy & Liz	All ongoing in prison as allowed and begin other things ASAP when released Liz will mail list of churches to Kathy by January 14
9. SUPPORTERS: Her family Liz Life Styles program Dawn & Lorenn Try new community mentor Linda to be introduced by Lorenn & Dawn – Linda can check in with her weekly and be a friend after her release	Kathy, Lorenn, Linda (potential mentor)	Lorenn will arrange for Kathy to meet Linda before she is released

THINGS TO DO	BY WHOM	COMPLETION DATE
10. OTHER: Kathy plans to file for a divorce. She will check what resources are available in the prison law library to file pro se and if she cannot prepare the legal proceedings on her own, she will contact Legal Aid for assistance filing for a divorce.	Kathy	Check what forms and information is available in the prison law library by January 15 and if she cannot obtain the necessary help there, she will contact Legal Aid by January 25 for its assistance.
11. FOLLOW UP CIRCLE: Re-Circle when her daughter Malia is on O'ahu for the summer if that happens or whenever Kathy needs a Circle after that within 6 months of release.	Kathy	Call Lorenn to schedule a follow up Circle 808 637-2385

Participants present with Kathy at her Circle: Lani granddaughter; Tess and Nanci daughters; daughters Jamie and Malia and parents provided information by telephone interview before the Circle was held; Liz incarcerated friend; Earl Larson prison counselor; Observer: Peter Tam, NYPD officer & CUNY college lecturer visiting Hawai'i, Facilitator: Lorenn Walker, Recorder: Dawn Slaten.

If you think anyone needs more help please call Lorenn at (808) 637-2385 or Dawn at (808) 383-5583.

Appendix G - Restorative Apology Letter Guidelines

Restorative Apology Letter Guidelines

These guidelines are based on www.apologyletter.org developed by Dr. Ben Furman, a psychiatrist from Finland, and Lorenn Walker, public health educator & former trial lawyer.

Directions: *[fill in [bracketed] information with the specifics facts of your situation and* **write out what is in bold***]*

[fill in date]   *[write your name & address on letter]*

Dear *[person's name you have hurt, and if you have hurt more than one person please write each person a separate letter]*:

[Describe what you did to the person you are writing this to that was hurtful, unfair, or wrong towards him/her]
I know I have hurt you with my action and I want you to know that I truly regret my behavior.

I have been thinking about what happened and I feel that I have learned a lesson. I have learned that: *[Describe what you have learned]*

I will never do anything similar again, to you or to anyone else. I am determined to deal differently with similar situations in the future.

In similar situations I will: *[Describe what you will do different in the future]*

I wish there was a way for me to make up to you what I did to you. If you have any ideas for how I might repair the harm I caused, I will try my best to do it. One possibility I thought of is: *[Describe what you might do to make it up to the person you have hurt]*

When I am able to, I am willing to listen to you and meet with you too if you wish.

Please let me know if you want to meet, or if there is anything else I can do to make things right. And please accept my sincere apologies.

Yours sincerely *[or love, aloha, etc. & your name]*

Revised Sept 2011

Appendix H - Example Behavioral Contract

Behavioral Contract
Between Kimo Smith and Julia & Ian Smith

Julia & Ian Smith agree to allow their son *Kimo Smith* to live with them in their Kahala home after he is released from Waiawa Correctional Facility under the following conditions:

1. Kimo agrees to remain clean and sober and not use any illegal drugs or drink any alcohol and if he does he will admit he relapsed and seek help;

2. Kimo agrees to not bring any people (i.e. friends, guests) to his parents' home (unless both parents meet the people and give Kimo their explicit permission);

3. Kimo agrees to attend church weekly;

4. Kimo agrees to help with his parents house maintenance i.e. yard work, etc.;

5. Kimo agrees to mow the lawn every other week and keep all the trees and plants trimmed and watered as needed;

6. Kimo agrees to wash all his own dishes within an hour after completing meals, and he will cook his own food;

7. Kimo agrees to pay rent of $250 a month as soon as he gets a job;

8. Kimo will apply for at least two jobs every weekday until he gets a job;

Kimo understands that if he violates any of these conditions he will have to move out of his parent's home and find another place to live within two hours of their request that he leave. **Kimo is only allowed to live with his parents as long as he abides by the above conditions, which may be altered with all parties consent.**

Signed:

_____   _____
Kimo Smith   Date   Julia Smith   Date

_____
Ian Smith   Date

Appendix I - Circle Participants Surveys

'Ohana (Family Member/Loved One) Survey

My name:_____ My age:_____ Date:_____

My relationship to Incarcerated person:_____ My Phone:_____

1. I believe the Huikahi Restorative Circle I participated in was:

❑ very positive ❑ positive ❑ mixed ❑ negative ❑ very negative

2. The Circle made me more optimistic about the incarcerated person's potential to stay out of prison:

❑ very positive ❑ positive ❑ mixed ❑ negative ❑ very negative

3. I believe the Transition Plan developed for the incarcerated person at the Circle is:

❑ very positive ❑ positive ❑ mixed ❑ negative ❑ very negative

4. I learned new information about the incarcerated person's strengths as a result of today's Circle:

❑ very positive ❑ positive ❑ mixed ❑ negative ❑ very negative

5. I think the Circle expanded the incarcerated person's social support:

❑ very positive ❑ positive ❑ mixed ❑ negative ❑ very negative

6. The Circle helped me reconcile with the incarcerated person:

❑ very positive ❑ positive ❑ mixed ❑ negative ❑ very negative

7. The Circle has helped me with forgiveness concerning the incarcerated person:

❑ very positive ❑ positive ❑ mixed ❑ negative ❑ very negative

8. I think the facilitator & recorder did good work with the Circle:

❑ very positive ❑ positive ❑ mixed ❑ negative ❑ very negative

9. The things I found most useful about the Circle were:

_____

10. The Circle could have been better if:

_____

_____

11. Additional comments or suggestions:

_____

Mahalo for your participation.

Incarcerated Person's Huikahi Survey

My name:_____Date:_____

My social security number's last four numbers:_____ Hawaiian? ❏ yes ❏ no

1. I believe the Huikahi Restorative Circle I participated in was:

❏ very positive   ❏ positive   ❏ mixed   ❏ negative   ❏ very negative

2. I believe the Circle was valuable in helping me make goals for the future:

❏ very positive   ❏ positive   ❏ mixed   ❏ negative   ❏ very negative

3. I believe the Transition Plan made at the Circle is:

❏ very positive   ❏ positive   ❏ mixed   ❏ negative   ❏ very negative

4. I learned something new about my strengths at today's Circle:

❏ very positive   ❏ positive   ❏ mixed   ❏ negative   ❏ very negative

5. I am more optimistic about my future and staying out of prison as a result of the Circle:

❏ very positive   ❏ positive   ❏ mixed   ❏ negative   ❏ very negative

6. I learned people care about me more than I thought before the Circle:

❏ very positive   ❏ positive   ❏ mixed   ❏ negative   ❏ very negative

7. The Circle helped me forgive myself and others:

❏ very positive   ❏ positive   ❏ mixed   ❏ negative   ❏ very negative

8. I think the facilitator & recorder did good work with the Circle:

❏ very positive   ❏ positive   ❏ mixed   ❏ negative   ❏ very negative

9. The things I found most useful about the Circle were:

_____

10. The Circle could have been better if:

_____

_____

11. Additional comments or suggestions:

_____

Mahalo for your participation.

Non-Related Huikahi Participant's Survey

My name:_____ Date:_____

My relationship to incarcerated person:_____ My Phone:_____

1. I believe the Huikahi Restorative Circle I participated in was:

❏ very positive ❏ positive ❏ neutral ❏ negative ❏ very negative

2. The Circle made me more optimistic about the incarcerated person's potential to stay out of prison:

❏ very positive ❏ positive ❏ neutral ❏ negative ❏ very negative

3. I believe the Transition Plan developed for the incarcerated person at the Circle is:

❏ very positive ❏ positive ❏ neutral ❏ negative ❏ very negative

4. I learned new information about the incarcerated person's strengths as a result of today's Circle:

❏ very positive ❏ positive ❏ neutral ❏ negative ❏ very negative

5. I think the Circle expanded the incarcerated person's social support:

❏ very positive ❏ positive ❏ neutral ❏ negative ❏ very negative

6. I believe the Circle helped 'Ohana members reconcile with the incarcerated person:

❏ very positive ❏ positive ❏ neutral ❏ negative ❏ very negative

7. The Circle has helped 'Ohana members with forgiveness concerning the incarcerated person:

❏ very positive ❏ positive ❏ neutral ❏ negative ❏ very negative

8. I think the facilitator & recorder did good work with the Circle:

❏ very positive ❏ positive ❏ neutral ❏ negative ❏ very negative

9. The things I found most useful about the Circle were:
_____
_____

10. The Circle could have been better if:
_____
_____

11. Additional comments or suggestions:
_____
_____

Mahalo for your participation.

Appendix J - Observer's Survey

Huikahi Restorative Circle Observer's Notations

Observer's Name: _____ **Date:** _____

Please note your observations for each part of the Circle that you watched.

1. **Opening:** What did you notice about the opening?

2. **Introductions**—any comments?

3. **Purpose & Guidelines:** How did the statement of purpose appear to be understood?

4. **Inmate's Proudest Accomplishment in Prison:** What did you notice when the incarcerated person discussed her accomplishments made in prison?

5. **Incarcerated person's Strengths:** If children of incarcerated person's strengths were discussed how do you think this part of the circle went?

How was the remaining part of the strengths or what people like about the incarcerated person, part of the circle in your opinion?

6. **Reconciliation—the group will address the three main restorative justice questions**—please comment on how each part of the dialogue went:

1. Who was affected by the incarcerated person's past behavior?

2. How were they affected?

3. What can be done to repair the harm?

Reconciliation plan with people harmed (related & unrelated) not attending the circle:
How did this part of the dialogue go?

What do you think of the agreement the group decided on for reconciliation?

7. Incarcerated person's Goals (what s/he wants different for future life): Comments?

8. Brainstorming Resources/Options for meeting incarcerated person's needs: What did you think worked best? Least? Any resources not addressed you think were necessary for a successful transition for this incarcerated person?

9. **Timelines Follow-up Circle Dates Established**: Comments?

10. Circle Closing: Comments?

What did the facilitator and recorder do well? What can they improve?

Any final comments about the Huikahi Circle process?

Mahalo for your observations. We work to continually improve the Circle process. We appreciate your thoughtfulness and comments.

Index

Citations

Baer, et al, 13, 74
Bazemore, G. 16, 43, 74
Berg, K. 7, 13, 16, 18, 29, 64, 65, 74
Berg & de Shazer, 16, 74
Braithwaite, J, 7, 14, 16, 44
Brantley, J, 29, 74
Dejong, P, 7, 18, 32, 65, 74
Dweck, C, 23, 25, 26, 74
Eglash, A, 43, 74
Ellis, A, 63, 74
Erikson, E, 20
Furman, B, 7, 47, 100, 101
Green, L, 63, 74
Hairston, CF, 13, 16, 74
Hawai'i State Legislature, 14, 74
Healey, K, 19, 74
Hogg & Cooper, 18, 74
Howerton, et al, 29, 74
Hwoschinsky, C, 62, 74
Interagency Council on Intermediate Sancitions, 21, 23, 75
Iverson, C, 40, 41, 75
Jenkins, A, 45
Jordan, M, 23, 75
Langer, E, 7, 20, 33, 75
Kabat-Zinn, J, 63, 75
Maruna, S, 7, 15, 16, 24, 25, 45, 74, 75
Mills, L, 7, 22, 75
Nouwen, H, 63, 75
Rose & Clear, 21, 75
Rumgay, J, 24, 74
Sakai, T, 7, 14, 16, 72, 76
Schwartz, S, & Boodell, D, 7, 17, 76
Seligman, M, 29, 75
Sherman & Stang, 16, 75
Shover, N, 25
Stockholm Prize in Criminality, 14, 75

Made in the USA
Charleston, SC
29 November 2011